An experienced guest lecturer, Mark W, Jones has distilled his adventures into a kind of Parkinson's Law of public speaking.

By now, in the course of his speaking engagements, almost everything that can go wrong *has* gone wrong – but usually (at least in retrospect) to his delectation.

Told with self-deprecating humour, *In A Manner of Speaking* is an A to Z guide for all groups who engage speakers and for the speakers themselves. The book maintains a logical progression despite the constraints of alphabetical order, moving steadily from the Athenaeum Club to the final Z is for Zizz.

From the wealth of anecdotes a complete picture emerges of the strange world of public speaking in Britain where there are at least 100,000 talks a year by the author's reckoning.

He himself has addressed many thousands of people and if Mark Jones's lectures are as entertaining as his book, it is no wonder he is so much in demand.

The text is copiously illustrated with cartoons by PHIL and the author's pen-and-ink sketches of the scenes of many of his adventures and misadventures, ranging from the gentlemen's club in London to the rural village hall.

☆　　☆　　☆

Mark W. Jones is a native of Yorkshire with a particular affection for York itself. His first book, *A Walk around the Snickelways of York,* has sold over 60,000 copies. This led to requests for 'A *Talk* Around the Snickelways of York' which has run to well over 200 performances. His adventures during these lectures have prompted his latest book.

Mark Jones, whose work has been featured on television and radio, has also published *The Complete Snickelways of York*. Married with three sons, he lives in the village of Bulmer, near Castle Howard.

Also by Mark W. Jones:
A Walk Around the Snickelways of York
The Complete Snickelways of York
The Foss Walk
The Time Traveller's Guide to York (co-author)

IN A MANNER
— OF —
SPEAKING

A Catalogue of Misadventure
for Speaker and Audience

Mark W. Jones

Temple House Books,
Sussex, England

Temple House Books
is an imprint of
the Book Guild Ltd.

Temple House Books
25 High Street,
Lewes, Sussex

First published 1992
© Mark W. Jones 1992

Set in Baskerville
Typesetting by Kudos Graphic,
Slinfold, West Sussex

Printed in Great Britain by
Antony Rowe Ltd.
Chippenham, Wiltshire.

A catalogue record for this book is
available from the British Library

ISBN 0 86332 816 4

To Bill
(who was short of
a Speaker)

Author's note on the Illustrations

PHIL'S cartoons, drawn as figments of his imagination as distinct from my recollection, illustrate and otherwise embroider the text with which they appear.

My sketches merely remind us from time to time that the real world still exists. In many cases these drawings have nothing to do with the text that preceeds or follows them; and you should not therefore read too much into their positioning.

MWJ

CONTENTS

ILLUSTRATIONS

(In order of Appearance)

Cartoons by Phil

St Peter's School, York

This book can be said to have started here. My first speaking experience, in aid of our local hospice, was in the spacious school hall: a "one-night stand" that led to unplanned consequences. Approaching the school's impressive portals, we are hardly surprised that its Patron Saint is shared with another impressive edifice just down the road: St. Peter's Cathedral, also known as York Minster.

INTRODUCTION

'MISADVENTURE: An unlucky event, misfortune . . . not due to crime or negligence'

(Collins English Dictionary)

This book happened by accident.

It occurred because the members of a certain male organization were pretty desperate for an after-dinner speaker for their annual dinner, at which members were to entertain their gracious and grateful Ladies. They also wished to be spared my standard offering of enlightenment about dark alleyways, which most of them knew all about anyhow, and did not wish their Ladies to know about.

'Cut out the visuals,' they said, 'and tell us about what went wrong.'

So it was necessary to look back through my somewhat crowded diary of speaking engagements during the last few years. Yes, a few things had gone wrong. In fact, come to think of it, several. Should they be remembered? Or would they be better consigned to oblivion? And how had I come to be involved in the first place?

I doubt whether many people on lists of speakers (other than politicians) actually said to themselves beforehand: 'I am going to be a speaker.' Usually they have their arm twisted by a speaker-finder who has been unable to fill in a gap in a painfully-compiled list of coming events; or by a fund-raising committee earnestly seeking some new means of persuading the public to contribute to their good cause.

So as with others, my first venture into speaking was unsought.

It had all begun soon after a small book of mine was published, about the Snickelways of York (defined as narrow places to walk along, leading from somewhere to somewhere else). Because of the difficulties of taking photographs in such places, I had chosen to illustrate the book with pen-and-ink drawings.

It was therefore to my surprise and apprehension that I was asked to do a public photographic slide-show on the subject, in aid of our local hospice. My camera had to be pressed into service, and eventually I reckoned that there was enough material to keep an audience quiet for an hour or so.

By a curious set of circumstances, the opportunity arose to carry out a trial run of the slide-show in an exceptional setting. It took place behind the defences of a US-manned ballistic missile early warning station Somewhere in England.

I would like to be able to say that this was because of the importance attached to my performance by the government of the United States. The truth was, however, that a sympathetic friend of ours had infiltrated the early warning station in the guise of an instructor. He had posed as tutor to a group of servicemen's wives. It was vital to them as good US citizens, he decided, that they should be thoroughly briefed on the dark alleyways of one of our cities.

Thus as guinea-pigs I was able to use forty members of a high-security organization under the name:

THE MENWITH HILL HAPPY HISTORY GROUP

This test–run having been conducted, I was as ready as could be expected for the main event, which took place shortly afterwards. It was attended by some 400 members of the public who had been persuaded to part with their entrance-money in aid of the hospice; and it was to be a one-night stand.

Instead it became what I suppose you would call an extended run.

All of which explains why, six years later, I found myself at the aforementioned dinner. The title chosen for me by the chairman was: 'Talking About Talking.'

In preparing my notes for this new subject, I had come to realize that the topic was far too varied and extensive to be covered in a half-hour dissertation, especially after an excellent meal and late at night. So I thought: 'If none of them walk out while I'm talking tonight, I might try writing a book about it.'

As it happened, some did walk out before I had even started.

Here nevertheless is my offering. It is written in order that my experiences might be shared with prospective speakers and audiences respectively, so that each might be better prepared for the other.

I have to admit that wandering through the alphabet is a pretty haphazard way of covering a subject that might have been more tidily packaged. But my talks file is itself haphazard. Successive engagements can be with a leukaemia research group and their friends tonight in a village hall, a fine arts society in a theatre next week, and a ladies luncheon club in a seaside hotel a few days later.

This is one of the many fascinations of talking. One meets such a remarkable range of contrasting organizations, people and circumstances.

If I tend to dwell upon the unexpected and the unintentional, it's because that's what happens. All of the events here are true (subject perhaps to a minor flight of memory here and there).

In many cases, confident that none of those involved will mind, I have identified the setting. In others I've withheld specific mention, not wishing to cause discomfort to those who have been kind enough to share with me my misadventures. After all, the definition with which we opened made it clear that when a misadventure happens, nobody's to blame.

If therefore in reading this book, you think you may have recognized something that rings a bell with you, you may be right. Or you may well decide, also quite rightly, that it never happened at all, *at least not when I was with you;* but even if it did occur, it wasn't anybody's fault. It just happened. And in happening, it served to add to our shared store of pleasurable recollections.

13

☆　　☆　　☆

Finally, the expected happens at least as often as the unexpected. So if you're a speaker-finder seeking a speaker to find; or if you're a member of the audience for whom a speaker has been found – don't worry. The unintended may never happen, and if it does, it will be all the more interesting.

With that conviction I offer this account of one speaker's experiences, in the hope that you may find something, somewhere, to help you through your next encounter with the unexpected. Perhaps you will then be able to savour your role all the more – whether you're speaking, listening, or just enjoying your well-earned state of somnolence.

St. Andrew's Church, Ingleby Greenhow

You'll need a good map to find Ingleby Greenhow - it's tucked away under the wooded northern folds of the Cleveland Hills. It's all the more surprising, therefore, to discover in this little village a 70-strong Lecture Society, in a modern, well-appointed hall, set into dense woodland. It's so overshadowed that I've had to take my pen-and-ink a little way up the lane, where nestles this exquisite and fascinating Norman church.

The Athenaeum Club, London

No drawing of mine can do proper justice to the magnificent frontage and heroic style of the Athenaeum, seen here from Waterloo Place, with Pall Mall in the background. Surmounting the entrance is the golden goddess Athena (who happens to bear a resemblance to Britannia, and indeed why not, Sir?). Presiding over all on his horse (and bearing no intentional resemblance to John Wayne) is, we are instructed,

EDWARDVS VII REX IMPERATUR 1901-1910

We therefore confer upon this picture a distinguished, classical shape, to be repeated on no other page.

 **is for ATHENAEUM**

The alphabet, being what it is, enables us to start with an air of distinction and respectability.

Not, I should make clear, that my sole speaking engagement there had anything to do with the wider membership of the Athenaeum Club, Pall Mall. Only one member of my audience was a member of the Club, and it was on the strength of this that the rest of us were allowed through its portals.

A is also, as it happens, for AMPS: the Athenaeum's Amps. It is the only building in which I have been totally unable to find a standard thirteen amp, flat-pin electrical socket into which to plug my equipment.

I searched in vain, high and low, above, below and behind the Athenaeum's substantial furniture. The only sockets were of a kind which went out of general use soon after World War Two: they required fifteen amp round-pin plugs. It was therefore necessary to go out and buy an Athenaeum-type plug, and a screwdriver with which to fit it.

But where? I was in Pall Mall, the heart of the land of clubs for gentlemen, and not known for its electrical stores, or indeed any other kind of store. The thought occurred to me that it might be worth trying Buckingham Palace, just up the road: they would surely have a venerable plug, fit for an Athenaean socket. But instead, recognizing that the Royal Family's need for their plug might be greater than mine, I decided to take the tube to Tottenham Court Road, capital of the empire of hi-fi retailing.

I was able to buy a screwdriver, but not, after an increasingly desperate search, an Athenaean plug. With time now running out, I realized that I would have to turn to the DIY man's last resort: to remove my plug, and wedge the bared wires into the Athenaean socket with a matchstick or two.

On my way back into the club I encountered a gentleman in authority, to whom, after establishing my meagre credentials, I mentioned my problem. Without a word he reached into his pocket, pulled out a bunch of keys and opened a drawer. From it he produced a lead, at one end of which was a thirteen amp socket, and at the other an Athenaean plug. It was the vital link between one age and another. 'We have to keep it locked up,' he explained, carefully handing it to me as a special concession. I might have had the Crown Jewels in my hand.

Why, I wondered as I bore it away, should it be necessary to keep this link with the twentieth century locked away from the members of the Athenaeum? Was it of such intrinsic value as an antique? Or could it be to discourage the Athenaeans from bringing in their own magic lanterns?

My hosts had kindly arranged that in addition to wining, dining and talking at the Athenaeum, I would also sleep there. The time came to turn in (the magic lead having served its purpose and been returned), and I retired to my room on one of the upper floors.

In the corridor outside the room I stumbled against an elegant reminder of times gone by: a Bath chair, resplendent with wickerwork back and sides, ornate handles and decorative swivelling wheels. It was thoughtfully provided, I assumed, for the use of members and their guests, as a helpful means of rapid self-transport to the far-distant bathroom.

But then I saw, carefully placed on the seat, the following uncompromising notice:

THIS CHAIR, BEING A RELIC, IS NOT TO BE USED.

I was reminded of the noticeboard somewhere in rural England with the sole inscription:

DO NOT THROW STONES AT THIS NOTICEBOARD.

Denied the use of the club's only Bath-chair, and unable to plug in his own magic lantern, the Athenaean must be a Spartan at heart.

☆　　☆　　☆

 **is for BREAKDOWN**

Of all the perils, projector-breakdown is the one most feared by the visually-aided speaker. It leaves him about as dignified and effective as a cyclist with a puncture, or an organist with failed bellows.

We must journey now to a Cumbrian village on the far side of Morecambe Bay. Because of its select and isolated location, you might expect that the village's Lecture Society would be sparse in membership, and accustomed to assemble on half a dozen benches in some spartan village hall. You would be, as I was, totally wrong.

The Lecture Society has no less than 350 attending members, and meets in a splendid auditorium. It has an expansive stage, row upon row of seats on the main floor, and more upstairs in the extensive balcony.

Usually I use my own projector and six-foot screen, which as we shall see later (see **PROJECTOR** and **SCREEN**) is adequate for audiences of up to about 150 people. But here, faced with a mega-audience, I was happy to accept the use of the society's equipment, which included a mega-screen and a mega-projector.

I was duly plugged-in to their system, attached to their microphone, and wired-up to their remote-control, which linked me with the far distant projector at the back of the hall.

As a back-up system, there were stationed at the projector an Operator and an Assistant Operator. If my electronic impulses for changing the slides became weakened by distance, the Operator would switch to Manual. If the Operator himself weakened, the Assistant Operator would take over. I was therefore instructed to allow for a moment's delay between

20

activation of slide-change and execution.

I felt equipped for a landing on the moon.

By that analogy, the launch, take-off and journey into orbit were entirely successful. It was not until preparation for landing was in sight – about two-thirds of the way into our flight – that the system ran into difficulties.

The next slide would not appear. I tried activating the slide-change several times, but the current picture remained obstinately on the screen. It was necessary to ad-lib for a moment, or two, or three, in order to allow the back-up systems to take over.

The Assistant Operator appeared, not at the projector, but at my side. 'Sorry, but we're having a bit of trouble,' he whispered, 'Soon have it going again – just keep on talking for a couple of minutes.'

So I kept on talking.

It is one thing to be faced with a total breakdown of the projector. At least you know where you stand. You activate your contingency plan. You can describe in words what your audience would have seen in pictures. Or you can switch to a totally different subject. (Once, in my earlier days, the Mayor and Rotarians of Gateshead were expecting me to present an after-lunch film about our Round Table's charity steam train. The projector bulb blew, I had no spare, and my audience had to be subjected instead to a discourse on Retail Price Maintenance in the Confectionery Industry. I'm still not certain that they were aware of the change).

Alternatively, you can simply bring proceedings to a sudden and merciful end.

But it is quite another matter to fill in time in the belief that the projector is about to re-start. You are firmly strapped in between the slide that you have, and the one that you expect. You can neither change course, nor stop and get off. So I had to continue ad-libbing, aware of the irrelevance of what I was saying. The audience was becoming increasingly restive.

Again the Assistant Operator appeared.

'Won't be long now,' he said.

Desperately I continued talking about this-and-that, here-and-there, now-and-again, any-moment-now . . .

Derwentwater

Usually, if he arrives too early for his engagement, the speaker may pass the time by pottering around nearby streets and shops. But not if he's going to speak in Keswick. Putting on his walking-boots, he takes the opportunity to enjoy a brisk walk up Cat Bells for the splendid view that the hill affords over Derwentwater. Beyond the lake, to the left, lies Keswick, with Blencathra in the distance.

After a full ten minutes that felt to me like as many hours, the Operator despatched his Assistant on his final mission, to bear me tidings of total defeat. I think he expected to be hit on the head. On the contrary, I shook his hand in sheer relief, and I suspect that he was applauded by the audience, who were by now more than ready for off.

So we never made it to the moon. I did my best to provide the audience with a verbal parachute, to bring them gently down to earth and out into the wet and windy night.

Yet even in the midst of disaster, some comfort was at hand. It came in the form of a lady whom I had never met before, who waited to speak to me afterwards.

'I always knew you Rowntree people had the gift of the gab,' she stated.

I was astonished. Here was I, a hundred miles from my former Taj Mahal in York, and far beyond the Sands of Lune. How did this lady come to know so well the secret of Rowntree's success?

'You see,' she continued authoritatively, 'my sister's brother-in-law was in Rowntree's before he became an M.P. . . . doing marketing.'

All was now explained. As I well knew, Rowntree Marketing Man was a distinctive species, even better endowed with the aforementioned gift than those of us with other persuasive tasks. But only one member of that species, and one well-known to me, had chosen to employ that gift in a House yet more distinguished than that in which I was standing. However circuitously, I now basked in his reflected glory.

But meanwhile, my audience was going home, frustrated. In restitution I offered to speak again for nothing: a benefit which I am sure my distinguished friend would readily have conferred upon his listeners elsewhere.

My offer still stands. It still awaits being taken up.

I cannot leave the subject of projector breakdown without recounting a remarkable sequel.

You will recall that the above incident took place beyond

Morecambe Bay. Three years later, having suffered no further such incident, I was revisiting Cumbria (perhaps a little further north than last time) to speak to another thriving rural lecture society, in another excellent hall, which had even been opened by the Queen herself. Again, I was linked up with the Society's own projector.

Having introduced my subject, I signalled for lights-out. They went out. I switched on my noises-off. They sounded. I pressed the button for the first slide to project. It didn't.

Or rather, it did; but it was so out-of-focus that my slide might have been a view of the gases surrounding Saturn, or the internal image of a cow's digestive system. The audience visibly reeled, perhaps resigning itself to a whole evening of unusual but incompetent photography.

At the back of the hall, the operator struggled manfully to adjust the focus. This only had the effect of making the blurred image move around the screen, and the audience reeled still further. With a resigned feeling of déjà-vu, I had to start ad-libbing before I had even started to speak. I was carrying on in Cumbria exactly where I'd left off. . . .

The operator continued with his heroic efforts at the back, while I continued to ad-lib. While I ad-libbed, I was desperately working out in my mind the logistics of retrieving my own projector from my car. It would have to be positioned in the middle of the hall . . . there was no centre aisle. . . I'd have to create one . . . half the audience and their chairs would have to shift sideways . . . their chairs were interlocked . . . 100 people to move . . . how long . . . how long . . . O, Lord . . .

Suddenly, the picture sprang into focus. The audience cheered resoundingly. With vast relief, I was able to stop ad-libbing, and projector and operator performed faultlessly thereafter.

But next time I'm invited to Cumbria (if ever), I think I'll install my own projector. *Before* I start to speak.

The Folk Hall, New Earswick

One of the real tests of a village hall must be: What does it look like <u>round the back</u>? Can any other hall compete with the Folk Hall, in this or any other respect? Built between 1907 and 1937 by the Joseph Rowntree Village Trust, it's always been far ahead of its time. It is the focal point for countless activities, whose participants come from near and far.

For this view I had to keep clear of a coachload of visitors, for whom the virtues of the Folk Hall were being extolled by their driver in (I think) <u>Dutch</u>!

 **is for CHAIRMAN**

The wise speaker never argues with the Chairman.

I use the term loosely, as *the person who is responsible for the control of the meeting.* He or she may however be addressed by another title, such as President. He or she may also be a Chairperson or a Chair, though I have not yet personally encountered one who wished to be thus addressed.

Most Chairmen do a very good job. They have a rapport with their members; they have done their homework on the speaker, whom they put at ease; they say the right things, and stop their members from saying the wrong things; and they heed the advice of their Secretary, whose job it is to know everything and everyone better than the Chairman does.

We will now indeed turn briefly to the Secretary. He or she is normally the speaker's contact beforehand. It is his or her job (among many other responsibilities) to sort out in advance the speaker's desires, whatever they may be.

My preferences, apart from wanting a socket (see ATHE-NAEUM) and a glass of something (see DRINK), are simple. They concern duration and questions:

It is helpful to know beforehand for how long one is to be allowed to speak. My preferred and full stint lasts nearly an hour-and-a-half. Most nocturnal organizations – those that meet in the evening – indulge me in this. But others, especially luncheon clubs, understandably prefer to keep me on a tighter rein.

I prefer to forego formal sessions of questions-and-answers. They tend to eat into speaking time. Further, it has been known for questioners to pose lengthy questions of no interest to

27

anyone else; and in any case, the audience has probably had enough of me by then. I therefore try instead to have a word with individual questioners aferwards.

So much for the arrangements that need to be sorted out beforehand. Now you should know of a train of resultant events in which I found myself one evening. You will then be prepared for the consequences, should it ever happen to you.

I was to speak to a certain long-established professional society (whose members all happened to be men) and their guests (who happened to be their ladies). The setting was a splendid room, whose walls were hung with original oil paintings of distinguished forebears. The arrangements for the evening had been agreed beforehand with the Secretary: I would give the full talk, after which there would be coffee in an outer room. There would not be a question-and-answer session.

Five minutes before I was due to start, I was introduced to the Chairman. 'How long are you going to take, then?' asked the Chairman.

'An hour and twenty-five minutes,' I replied, helpfully.

'Oh heck,' he said, 'we can't have *that*.'

Somewhat put-out, I explained that the Secretary and I had discussed and agreed upon the arrangements.

'No,' said the Chairman, 'we've got to stick to our procedures. You speak for an hour – that'll be quite enough – then coffee, then back for questions-and-answers, and we'll all be out by a quarter-to-ten.'

I sought in vain for a compromise, but to no avail. There was just time for me to ask the surprised Secretary to rearrange our arrangements, and the meeting began.

'Tonight,' said the Chairman, 'we have Mr . . . er . . . to speak to us about . . . er . . . I can't remember what he's going to talk about, but he'll explain all that. But before he starts, let me give you all a warning. If any of you want to leave early, you'll have to be out by eight o'clock . . .' (it was now half-past-seven) '. . . because the outside door will be locked at eight, and I've got the only key.'

Never before, and never since, have I enjoyed a physically

captive audience. None did attempt to make their escape during the first half hour. I gave my abbreviated talk in the belief that they were locked in to ensure that they heard me through. Later however I learned that it was because the doorman wished to catch an early train home soon after eight o'clock.

There followed coffee, by the end of which the audience had clearly lost its enthusiasm for returning for questions. They were finally released, as prescribed, at a quarter-to-ten.

But the lock on the exit-door had a further role to play.

My ten-piece equipment, which weighs a hundredweight and three-quarters (see OBSTACLE), takes a good quarter of an hour to pack up. Two kind members of the audience stayed behind to help me, and finally we arrived in the entrance-hall. It was totally deserted.

We made for the exit-door. It was securely locked against us. Try as we might, we couldn't get out.

We thought of phoning the police or the fire brigade, but there was no accessible phone. We considered abandoning my equipment and climbing out of a window; but the only window we could reach involved a twenty-foot drop, with the risk of being impaled on the handsome wrought iron railings surrounding the building. As a last resort, we crowded ourselves and my equipment into a lift, and pressed the basement button, in the belief that there would be a lower exit. The lift descended into the depths, until at last we stopped with a jerk.

The lift doors slid open, to confront us with what appeared to be a pitch-black void. We knew that we must have reached the basement because of the all-pervading smell of fust, dust and steam pipes. The feeble light of my projection pointing-torch shone its arrow, not into a void, but into a black binliner: one of dozens, stacked from floor to ceiling. Further inspection with the pointing-arrow revealed the binliners to be stuffed with presumably secret documents, all carefully shredded.

We had no choice but to tunnel our way through this underground mountain of discarded time and resource, to find ourselves at the foot a narrow steps leading steeply upwards. Upwards we struggled through the darkness, still with my

29

equipment, until finally we stumbled against the push bar of an emergency exit-door.

Freedom! But not until, still with my equipment, we had descended an external flight of steps to the dimly-lit street below, and into the arms of the distraught wife of one of my fellow-escapers, who had given up all thought of ever seeing her husband again.

The wise speaker never argues with the Chairman.

 **is also for COFFEE**

Coffee is the great opiate of the people who constitute your audiences. It may be taken at any time of day, on the slightest pretext, on one or more of the following occasions:

- Preceding and/or following men's meetings in the morning
- Long preceding and/or immediately preceding, accompanying and sometimes following ladies' luncheon meetings
- Following men's lunchtime meetings
- Preceding and following ladies' afternoon meetings
- Following mixed-sex dinners
- In the interval of mixed-sex evening meetings and/or following ladies' and/or mixed-sex evening meetings.

It will be noted that the sexes do not usually mix for coffee until the evening. Ladies are usually too busy to meet in the morning, and men are much too busy to meet in the afternoon, or cannot keep awake (see **SEX**). The above list applies primarily to weekdays. It does not include the mixing of the sexes that takes place on Saturday afternoons, notably among members of the National Trust, who normally take coffee after they have mixed.

The physical circumstances in which coffee is consumed vary considerably:

- At men's morning meetings, it is usually taken standing up at the back of the church hall in which they meet, such being the most cost-effective accommodation that they can find. It is often prepared and served by their wives, who are confined to

31

the church hall kitchen, where there is always a smell of gas.

- Coffee and other drinks before and after a ladies' luncheon are usually taken sitting down, in the comfortable furnishings and surroundings of the high-class establishments in which they meet. It is prepared and served not by their husbands (who are much too busy) but by paid and uniformed hotel staff.
- Coffee that follows a meal is served at the table while the speaker is sorting out his equipment, and is usually cold by the time he drinks his.
- Evening meetings can present the most severe coffee problems, on which we shall now concentrate.

Evening meetings are often attended by friends, relations and members of the public. They are there, not so much because they wish to hear the speaker, but in order to contribute money to the excellent cause to which the organizers have committed themselves. Coffee-and-biscuits is often advertised as one of the attractions, and in exchange the audience is usually invited to pay a modicum extra.

It is therefore imperative that, come what may, all members of the audience receive the coffee-and-biscuits to which they are entitled. This usually happens after the speaker has finished speaking, though it can happen when he is only half-way through, either by design or because the boiler has boiled more quickly than expected.

The accommodation is often too limited to allow members of the audience to get up and walk about with their coffee; still less to go elsewhere. It is therefore served to them while they remain on their chairs. Brimming and steaming cups-and-saucers are borne on trays down the centre aisle, and passed from hand to hand along the rows. Those who are sitting at the far ends therefore find that more of their coffee is in the saucer than in the cup.

Perhaps my most spectacular coffee experience occurred in a village hall in which the audience was, shall we say, close to the Fire Regulations Limit. My contribution was over for the evening, and some of us were standing chatting somewhere at the front, where there was room to move. Coffee was being served by the method outlined above.

Suddenly, from half-way down the hall, there was a thunderous crash. I realized with some alarm that the sound came from the precise location of my projector and slides, which were still in position.

A member of the audience had unwittingly knocked a full tray out of the hands of the lady serving the coffee-and-biscuits. A great tide of coffee swept the centre aisle, swirling around the shattered remains of a dozen cups and saucers and broken biscuits. The flood also engulfed my slide-magazines under the projector-stand along with 150 colour-slides which had just been projected.

Through my mind rushed a comparable flood of fears. Gone forever would be the slides, with thirty unfulfilled speaking engagements ahead. Gone would be my hard-back book, for which the publisher was awaiting the slides for processing into colour-plates. Gone would be the perils and pleasures of life as a speaker. Gone, all gone. . .

But with the characteristic efficiency of organizing committees everywhere, an excellent flood-relief operation swung into action. In no time the slides had been fished out of the coffee and sandwiched flat between teatowels, while the magazines were flushed out under the kitchen tap. With the worst of the spillage removed from the slides, I was able to reload them temporarily into the magazines and rush them home, disordered but rescued from death-by-drowning.

Once home, through the small hours, my wife and I were able to complete the salvage operation. Fortunately all of the slides were fully-mounted, with the sensitive transparencies protected by layers of glass and set in plastic mounts. Each slide had to be dismantled. The residual coffee, which had begun to seep in at the edges, was wiped away, the glass cleaned, and the slides reassembled. Only the aroma of the coffee remained.

By the following evening, when my next talk was due, the slides had all been treated. But there remained a critical doubt:

33

Would they withstand the heat of the projector? I would have to wait and see . . .

I need not have worried. Not only were the slides undamaged, but it was the first time that I had projected so many freshly-cleaned slides in succession. I was so pleased with the result that I soon polished up the remaining fifty which had escaped the coffee deluge. To add to this happy outcome, my wife and I were surprised and grateful the following day to receive from my hosts a delightful delivery of fresh flowers, which brightened the February day and far outshone any lingering scent of coffee.

I would not however recommend the coffee treatment as a means of prompting the speaker to clean up his slides. It causes too many nice people too much overnight anguish.

☆   ☆   ☆

 **is for DRINK**

Apart from whatever the audience may be served, it is important for the speaker to have access to drink, in case he or she becomes hoarse, parched or overheated.

I have found it helpful to specify in advance, and in writing, my liking for a glass or two of water to hand. Even so, it can sometimes be difficult for the organizers to rustle up a suitable vessel. Often at the last minute, a feverish hunt begins through every back room, and through chests, cupboards and cabinets.

Ideally, the hunt ends not only with a tumbler but with a filled jug of water as well. But I have on occasion been offered many vessels, ranging from a medicine-measure, through sherry, wine and whisky glasses, teacups and beakers, to a milk jug and a one-pint beer glass.

The most original vessel of all, however, was pressed into use in a large school hall, at a major evening fund-raising event for the NSPCC. The vessel-hunt was in full cry, with only a few minutes to go. Despair set in when it was discovered that every crockery cupboard in the school was locked. Then one of the resourceful organizers had an inspiration: 'Let's try the Craft Room!' she suggested, and disappeared down the corridor. She returned some time later, bearing triumphantly a foot-high, two-handled earthenware vase (slightly misshapen), into which she had coaxed a modicum of water from the taps in the infant girls' toilets. Thus was my thirst slaked at intervals through the evening, even though it took two hands to do it.

I have carefully referred to the content of these many and varied vessels as water. This it usually is, even though the audience may believe otherwise. Ocasionally however, especially

35

where no water-tap can be found, recourse is made to orange-juice, lager, wine and, *in extremis*, gin.

The Priory, Orpington, Kent

This is not, as you might expect, the private residence of some benefactor, in aid of whose good cause the speaker is pontificating within. It is the Orpington Public Library, and I doubt whether any other public library in the land is housed in such attractive surrounds. Here also meets the Orpington Camera Club, whose members kindly invited one speaker to talk about a subject far beyond their normal pastures.

Museum of Army Transport, Beverley

When in search of your audience, you don't normally expect to have to circumnavigate a Centurion Mark V tank ("Ann", 1944) and the world's smallest standard-gauge steam loco ("Gazelle", 1893). These, and many other interesting distractions, confront you when you're looking for the Beverley Decorative and Fine Arts Society. You suddenly find them beyond the exhibits, in an immaculate 150-seat theatre. The speaker operates everything within by push-button remote control, including surprising effects with the house-lights.

 **is for ENJOYMENT AND OTHERWISE**

This section is not necessarily about misadventure. It is more an attempt to analyse why it is that people in groups invite other people to go and talk to them.

The avowed aims and objects of their groups are diverse, ranging from horticulture to alternative medicine, and from the uses of gas to the arrangement of flowers. Are there any common factors?

I know of one, for a start. Most groups are, with varying degrees of determination, trying to find a speaker: furthermore, not merely one speaker for one date, but one of a series lasting into infinity. Their task is therefore endless. It is not surprising that a speaking small-fry like myself is sometimes netted in these much-fished waters.

For interest, I did an analysis after my 200th talk of what I *believed* to be the expectations of each of the groups that had invited me. Whether these expectations were satisfied is a different matter. But here, under three brief headings, are my assumptions:

Enjoyment	55%
Enlightenment	25%
Enrichment	20%

Enjoyment: (55%)

I believe this to be the main objective of the groups which meet regularly. They spread their speaker net over a wide range of topics. They may indeed be enlightened by some of their speakers, but they are not ashamed to enjoy themselves either. They probably come primarily to enjoy each other's company, and the speaker's subject and performance are incidental to that process.

This motive is probably shared with an unexpected grouping of professional organizations. Their work is associated with human or animal health, and they presumably feel the need to take their minds off this from time to time. I have in mind members of the Royal Society of Midwives, the Pharmaceutical Society, the Friends of the Veterinary Benevolent Fund, and the International Federation of Healing.

Enlightenment: (25%)

This is what people go out in search of who want to know more, or do something better, than they do already.

Usually they are members of societies with a defined specialized interest, and they try to engage speakers who fit into that mould. They search for earnestness rather than pleasure, but if they enjoy being earnest along the way, so much the better. They are therefore willing to stretch a point or two to take in the dark alleys as well as the shining highways of cultural improvement. Sometimes the dividing-line is a fine one.

Included here are history societies, literary societies, camera clubs, lecture societies, fine arts societies and adult education groups.

Enrichment: (20%)

By this I do not mean people filling their own pockets: the very opposite.

These are the organizations and societies who organize special events to raise funds for charities and other good causes, ranging from the big national charities to small groups assiduously trying to repair their village hall or bring help or comfort to those who most need it. I never cease to be surprised at the number of people, from all walks of life, who continue to give vast amounts of their time and effort in voluntary support groups. Such groups are an essential part of the fabric of our society.

I'm sure that, in doing so, they also derive a lot of enjoyment and enlightenment, but if so, it will be secondary in their minds to their main purpose. The total funds raised in this way must be prodigious. Those who have organized my talks alone – and as we have seen, I am but a small fish – have raised associated sums that run into five figures.

Conclusion

In round terms, about half of the groups who ask me along to speak are in search of enjoyment, with the remainder roughly equally divided between those seeking enlightenment and those doing good. Somehow this seems to me to be a very encouraging reflection of our society as a whole.

I can't leave the enjoyment of the audiences, however without emphasising my own. The misadventures, often themselves enjoyable in their own peculiar fashion, are far outnumbered by a rich store of pleasures. I could give you many examples. Here are but two, each quite different in nature:

Recently I spent an enjoyable evening with a coronary support group, whose membership consists of those who have suffered severe heart problems, and most of whom have had at least one major operation. Their group was formed only two years earlier, with a membership of twelve. Now, with their partners, their numbers had increased to over 100.

I had expected to find an audience that was subdued and perhaps a little strained, and for very understandable reasons. How wrong I was! I cannot remember, anywhere, having come across a stronger sense of warmth, fellowship, responsiveness and sheer joy of living.

The experience left me with a feeling of admiration, both for the members of the medical profession, and for those who had responded so well to their skills. I also felt humility at how one takes good health for granted.

By contrast, many of the pleasures last for only fleeting moments, but etch themselves into one's memory.

One evening I happened to be making my way to speak to the Yorkshire Countrywomen's Association branch at Sleights, in the North Yorkshire valley of Eskdale. The road takes one across the high, wide sweep of the lovely North York Moors, and I was to witness a remarkable sunset.

The sky, a magnificent expanse of merging blues, yellows, greens and reds, swept down to the heather-covered moors, still deep purple in the twilight. I breasted the northern edge of the hills and started down Blue Bank; what main-road steep hill has a lovelier and more appropriate name? In the dusk ahead and below twinkled the lights of the little fishing town of Whitby, with its ruined abbey silhouetted against the silver sea that stretched out to meet the darkening eastern horizon.

For me, a memorable and enriching experience – and only one of many.

Whitby

My earliest remembered childhood holiday was in Whitby. It's a town of extraordinary contrasts. Garish fun-fairs sit cheek-by-jowl with the otherwise attractive and timeless fish-quay. On the opposite side of the harbour are the tightly-packed terraces of fishermen's cottages, overlooked by the austere ruins of St. Hilda's Abbey on the cliff-top. To the right, the River Esk comes down from the moors. Below us, the contented holidaymakers sit round the silent band-stand, enjoying instead the screaming of the gulls. The speaker seldom shares this pleasure, as he is usually confined to hotels on the North Cliff.

 **is for FEES**

The juxtaposition of this subject with the previous one is regrettable but unavoidable, and is dictated solely by the alphabet.

When I was first asked what was my fee for speaking, I was at a loss. So I sought guidance from a friend, whose talks have stimulated the interest of thousands in the fascinations of our city.

'Mark,' he said 'you *must* charge a fee: EVEN TO ROTARY.'

Not appreciating at the time the significance of his last remark, I sat down to do some simple arithmetic.

The formula I devised was based on how much my talking was worth per head per hour to whoever was (or was not) listening. This assessment worked out at around 50p per person for an hour of listening (or not) to me.

Expressed as a rate per head, this equates to one-sixtieth of the hourly rate charged by my garage for draining the dirty oil out of my sump. So I think it must be about right.

It does not of course take into account non-chargeable time spent loading equipment into the car; driving to the speaking-place; unloading it at the speaking-place; setting it up; dismantling it; reloading the car; driving home; and re-unloading the car on getting back home. In order to spend one hour speaking, one must expect to spend at least four hours between leaving home and getting back.

Largely because of this time element I request a minimum audience of sixty.

Some speakers I know charge considerably higher fees, and I'm sure they are worth it. They each have to weigh up how

44

much their time is worth to them personally, and how much they would rather be doing something else instead.

So much for the high finance. Now for its acceptability.

It is notable that women's organizations invariably seem to regard the fee as fair and acceptable, and sometimes even insist on making it more. The same is generally true of mixed organizations (see SEX). I regret to say however that, with some notable exceptions, this cannot generally be said of all-male events. The more business-orientated men are, the more resistant they tend to become to the payment of fees.

'We have some very old members, y'know, so we have to keep the subscription down,' it has been said. Sometimes I wonder whether the possibility has been considered of cross-subsidisation of the weaker parts of the business enterprise.

Perhaps men's organizations consider it enough of a privilege for the speaker to be allowed to speak for an-hour-and-a-half without being interrupted. As I well recollect, this privilege is totally unknown in business. And maybe they further consider that, after all, this fellow ought to have more useful things to do with his time than standing there talking his head off. Finally (as I have been specifically informed by a men's speakers' secretary), their members can't be expected to keep awake for more than half-an-hour, and how can you expect them to pay you for talking to them in their sleep?

Maybe they are quite right. Maybe it all boils down to cost-effectiveness. The statistical effect can be found much later, under SEX.

☆   ☆   ☆

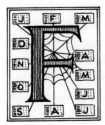 **is also for FREQUENCY**

As a well-organized speaker, you will of course arrange your winter programme so that:

a You speak neither more nor less often than you wish
b Your speaking engagements are evenly-spaced with each other, and with your other commitments
c You are always free of speaking engagements when you wish to do something else

You will also find that this is totally impossible.

You can't say: 'I propose to speak to you, and I'm coming on such-and-such a date. By ready to welcome me.' Your speaking diary is entirely governed by who asks you to speak, and when. It's true that usually you are offered some choice of date; but it will usually be on a certain night of the week, and at a certain time.

An analysis of my diary for the last five years shows that, by some strange alchemy and not by design, my speaking engagements from October to May inclusive have without exception numbered between thirty-three and thirty-seven each year. This averages almost exactly one a week, which is a nice, gentlemanly pattern. But the distribution is far from gentlemanly.

October is always the most crowded month. Doubtless it has something to do with the long lay-off: when societies, having escaped speakers through the long summer months, feel that they will need to subject themselves again to this manifestation of life's trials. Next in demand comes March, presumably because they decide that they'd better get you out of the way before summer comes.

But even within that pattern, my diary is hopelessly irregular. Four times in a week is not uncommon, and three times in twenty-four hours is not unknown. The saving grace is that at least you know well in advance what to expect. Most bookings are at least six months ahead, and this often extends to a year or eighteen months.

Perhaps my most crowded moments, however, came out of the blue, when I was due to speak to members of the Third Age at their national conference. The Third Age is a splendid euphemism for those of us who, whilst reluctantly acknowledging that we are a bit beyond The Middle Age, are even more reluctant to be thought of as The Elderly.

By its very nature, the conference offers to its members a wide range of Creative Activities. On the evening of my appearance therefore, my talk was only one of three alternatives. In the large hall was Country Dancing, for the Physically Creative. In a smaller hall was Poetry Reading, for the Mentally Creative. My talk, obviously and appropriately, was for the Physically and Mentally Uncreative minority, in the committee room.

But that evening, many Creative conference members were obviously exhausted by earlier creative activities, and the

committee room was overflowing well before my starting-time. A creative riot threatened to develop. There was no choice but to hurriedly announce my first-ever Second House, to take place an-hour-and-a-half later.

By the time the first house was over, the country dancers and poetry readers had ceased their creativity, and had joined the Uncreative Overflow. The second house therefore took place under conditions of considerable privation for the audience.

I would not therefore recommend a speaking frequency of twice a night. That's best left to the acting profession, and to those who are more creative than I.

 **is for GARB**

'GARB: Clothes, esp. the distinctive attire of an occupation or profession, eg clerical garb.
(16th Cent. from Old French garbe, graceful contour)'
(Collins English Dictionary)

In searching for a suitable heading for this section, I was surprised to find (as perhaps you were) that the word GARB is not derogatory slang for the clothes worn by people of whom one disapproves. On the contrary, it is wholly respectful, of noble antecedents, and entirely appropriate to head these notes on what the speaker should wear.

Not that there is a particular form of distinctive attire available to your average speaker (unless he happens to be a Mister Speaker in the Commons, in which case he will wear very fancy garb indeed). For the rest of us, the essential requirement is simply to wear the right garb at the right time. If it gives us a graceful contour, so much the better, though this is often not attainable.

At this point I must apologize to lady speakers. I would not presume to offer them guidance, even if I could. They will always know what to wear, and they will always ensure that what they wear is not what anyone else is wearing.

For male speakers, the objective is precisely the opposite: you must wear whatever the men in your audience will be wearing. In other words, you must look like one of them. Otherwise you will alienate them by appearing either lacking in respect or eccentric, as the case may be. It is necessary therefore to have a variety of garb available, and to choose what is appropriate to the occasion.

Here is my ready-reckoner:

Type of audience	Garb of Speaker
Ladies in the morning	Suit
Men in the morning	Jacket, old
Ladies at lunchtime	Suit
Anyone in the afternoon	Jacket, comfortable
Evening event, without dinner	Jacket, well-cut
Evening event, with dinner	Suit
Evening event, fastidious	Dinner jacket
Photography clubs, walking clubs (any time)	Pullover
Students, academics (any time)	Pullover, old
All of the above (lights out, talk in progress)	Shirt sleeves

Some groups spell out their sartorial requirements. It is, for instance, one of the long-established rules of the Hull Literary and Philosophical Society that the speaker shall wear formal dress. This is communicated to him in advance, in a helpful set of *Notes for Speakers*. (As it happens, the society's rules also specify that the speaker shall speak for sixty minutes precisely; that there shall be no questions; and that there shall be no vote of thanks). (As it also happens, formal dress can present its own peculiar problems: see NECKWEAR).

In the absence of such precommunicated rules, you can of course ask the organizer what you should wear. I was recently required to speak at a charity dinner, and shortly beforehand found myself wondering whether this, too, would be a dinner-jacket affair. I rang the lady who had arranged the event, and asked her what the other men would be wearing.

There was a strange sound at the other end, followed by a graceful apology:

'I'm sorry – didn't I explain? There won't be any men there at all, so it doesn't matter what you wear.'

Not quite sure whether I was a man or not, I was left to ponder, with this freedom of choice, what to pick from my ready-reckoner chart. In the end I settled for my let's-pretend-it's-summer jacket, only to find that the impeccable turn-out of my audience would have merited nothing less than white tie and tails.

Come to think of it, there would be a lot to be said for having a distinctive attire for speakers everywhere. You wouldn't then have to think about what you were going to wear. Just reach inside the cupboard, and throw it on. But what?

Not so very long ago there used to exist an item of attire known as a SMOKING JACKET, defined by Collins as:

'. . . a man's comfortable jacket of velvet etc, closed by a tie belt or fastenings, worn at home.'

I can think of nothing better than this distinctive but comfortable jacket. Nobody wears one these days for smoking: they can get on with their vice without one. So let's revive the smoking jacket as the speaking jacket, to be worn only when speaking, and never at home.

After all, why should church dignitaries, judges and senior academics have a monopoly of fancy dress to denote their occupation?

St. Chad's Church, Far Headingley

From boyhood years, I can still hear the mellow pealing of the bells of St. Chad's on sunlit summer evenings. The tall spire of this vast outer-suburban church forms an impressive landmark, rising above the long, graceful avenue of trees in its own substantial parkland. Opposite, in my day, was its surprising neighbour: the Far Headingley Tramsheds, to which all the best trams in Leeds came clanking home to roost at night. Close by, tonight's speaker in the Parish Centre need not compete with the grinding of the trams: only with the subdued and soulless throb of the buses that long ago replaced them.

 **is also for GIFTED CHILD**

If I fail to keep awake such audiences of adult men as may be willing to give me a hearing (see FEES), the same cannot be said of one branch of a national organization for The Gifted Child.

The organization exists to serve the special needs of children of such advanced intelligence that they find it difficult to identify with others in their environment who learn more slowly. Special stimulating and challenging events are therefore organized for them, in order to stretch their unusual abilities. I am not sure by what means they are recognized as gifted, but their parents are in no doubt.

It was therefore something of an honour and a challenge to be invited to speak to this group. True, I would have to be on my mettle. I envisaged fifty junior Mensa members listening raptly to my every word, and challenging my views and comments at every twist and turn. It was therefore not without some trepidation that I set up my equipment, appropriately enough in a lecture room designed for post-graduate students. My starting-time with the gifted children was approaching.

With ten minutes to go no one had arrived. I put this down to the children's gift of not wasting their time by arriving anywhere any earlier than necessary.

With five minutes to go, I was still the only person in the building apart from the caretaker. An unpleasant thought occurred to me. Had I got the date wrong? It was too late now to check.

Starting-time arrived, and there was still no sign of an audience.

After another five minutes I began to pack up.

After another ten minutes the audience arrived.

It consisted of thirteen people: Eight adults and their five gifted children. At least, I assume that all five were gifted, because no one told me that any of them were not. They ranged in age from three to fifteen. I did not attempt to rationalize the ratio or relationship of adults to children. No doubt it will have figured in a Mensa test-paper.

I began to speak. It was not easy, because the youngest Gifted Child (the capital letters are used to distinguish him from the other gifted children, whose behaviour was exemplary) was running round the room, shouting.

After some time however I was able to make myself heard again: the shouting Gifted Child had cleverly worked out how to get out of the room, and had run shouting down the corridor, pursued by a man whom I assumed to be his father.

In the silence that followed, the intelligent questions started to flow from the remaining four children.

But then normal service was again interrupted. The shouting Gifted Child's voice was approaching, this time from a different direction. Another door burst open, and in rushed the child, followed some time later by his breathless father, who leaned exhausted against the door. One of the other parents sprang to man the unguarded door.

Thus was the shouting Gifted Child contained within the lecture room. He continued however both to shout and to run. My contribution was lost to the ears of the audience, who had to be content with slides unaccompanied by commentary.

Eventually the father of the Gifted Child stepped forward, indicating that he would like to speak to me.

'Would you like me to take him out?' he asked.

I was so impressed by this gesture of consideration for speaker and audience that after due thought for some time, at least two milliseconds, I accepted the suggestion. For my part, I considerately suggested that the remaining gifted (but exemplary) children might wish to go the same way, and they rapidly did, along with their parents.

But it would be a pity if this isolated experience of mine were to deter others, or for that matter myself, from accepting any future challenge to speak to gifted children. The gift of remarkable ability can undoubtedly be a very mixed blessing both to child and parent; and it must be in the interests of us all that such gifts should be harnessed to the benefit of society as a whole. If we can help by trying to meet such children on their own terms now and again, so much the better.

I have however equipped myself with a secret weapon, in case I fail the test in future (see POINTER).

 **is for HANDBAG**

This is an object positioned on a chair by a member of a ladies' luncheon club well before luncheon, in order to ensure that it is beside or opposite other handbags of the requisite acquaintance and credentials. Hence the verb

> 'BAG *vb, tr. Brit. informal:*
> '*to reserve or secure* the right to do or have something'
>
> (Collins English Dictionary)

Sometimes, instead, some other cherished personal possession may be used for this purpose, such as an initialled handkerchief, a visiting card or a shopping bag bearing the Harrod's imprint. In this context, such objects all come under the species HANDBAG, and are interchangeable in the references below.

For reasons explained later under LUNCHEON MEETING, I find it necessary to arrive very early for such meetings. But however early I arrive, it sometimes happens that some handbags are already in position, and others will continue to drop quietly into place while I am setting up my equipment or attempting to do so.

This is because of a rule that I have learned, and not only among ladies, and not only at lunchtime:

People like to sit with the people with whom they like to sit.

How many of us go out of our way to sit with someone

56

unknown to us? Or with someone who is not unknown to us, but not quite so well known to us as those we sit with if we can?

If we do not habitually seek out the company of those whom we know less well, it is not that we are unsociable. It is simply because most of us are naturally modest, reserved, discerning, mutually respectful, and not given to garrulous exchange with whoever we might find ourselves next to regardless of who they are.

This is a characteristic unique to these shores: hence the dictionary's attribution of the verb BAG. As Collins reminds us, the word is

trad. British

I have discussed this characteristic frequently during luncheon, with office-holders and other members whose hospitality and company I always enjoy. They invariably say they wish that people knew each other better, and sometimes they try to do something about it.

Some luncheon clubs have therefore introduced rules forbidding Bagging. Indeed, I happened to be present on the very occasion on which one president announced the future banning of this practice, and you could have cut the silence with a nail-file.

Where such a rule has been introduced, some members may nevertheless stand, move and sit in the same pattern in relation to each other as would otherwise have been formed by their handbags. Others have occasionally been known to arrive not for lunch but for morning coffee, and have happened to remain in their places until the table has been reset for lunch.

But occasionally a club has courageously introduced what I will call the Grand Sitdown Draw. Each table-place is numbered, and each member on arrival draws a number out of a hat, and when the time comes, sits at that place.

Thus everyone knows everyone else, no one worries where they sit, and new friendships can develop beyond the confines of the luncheon-table.

Except, as I think I might once have happened to notice, when someone has quietly moved the place-numbers around.

The Black Swan, Helmsley

We enjoy any excuse to visit Helmsley, set between the Howardian Hills and the North Yorkshire Moors. Overlooked by its castle, it combines antiquity with aristocracy (nearby Duncombe Park, now open to the public, is the seat of Lord Faversham). The shopping is distinctly upmarket, though the market-square has its own down-to-earth pleasures – if you can find a parking-space. In the Black Swan, the Helmsley Ladies' Luncheon Club holds its meetings in low-ceilinged and deeply-carpeted ambience.

Halifax

When you venture to Halifax, this is what lies before you – or some of it. The panorama refuses to be reduced to smaller dimensions. You don't need a helicopter for this view. Just catch the local bus up the road to Southowram.

Halifax is a remarkable mixture of old and new, of industry and leisure, of grime and sparkle, of hills and valleys – and all held together by the sheer character of the place. Hills. You can't escape them. Your brake linings will last you only half as long as anywhere else.

In this picture, on the extreme left beyond the white spire, is the great quadrangle of the 18th-Century Piece Hall, where the weavers brought their cloth to be sold and exchanged. In the centre is the parish church (15th Cent.), with its square tower. Beyond that is the distinctive mill chimney – one of a dwindling number – of the former splendid Crossley carpet

factory, Dean Clough, now a hive of small industries. From the right swoops in the link road from the M-62, on a fly-over above the older bridge.

But there's much more. Out of the picture, to the left, are the awesome 1970s head-quarters of the Halifax Building Society; and the Mackintosh factory, the home of Quality Street and other deservedly famed goodies. I must ask my friends there to rest content with the tip of their chimney, which I've squeezed into the left foreground

Above and beyond rise the wild Pennines, on whose slopes grazed the sheep that gave rise to the once-thriving woollen industry. Without them, there would have been no Halifax as we know it; no YMCA building; and no speaker struggling up its distinctive staircases somewhere in the midst of it all.

 **is also for HULL**

From Hell, Hull and Halifax
May The Good Lord Deliver us.

(Old Saw)

Elsewhere on these pages we specifically mention Halifax, so it is only right and proper now to take a brief look, if not at Hell, then at Hull.

In defiance of the Old Saw, the speaker has frequently enjoyed delivering himself both to Halifax and to Hull. But for the stranger, self-delivery to Hull can have its problems.

When you drive to Hull you will naturally look for the road signs pointing to Hull. You will not be disappointed. There they are, one after another, saying: **HULL**.

But on reaching the approaches to that proud city, you will encounter a much larger roadside sign. It bears the following information:

WELCOME TO KINGSTON UPON HULL

Wilcom in
Bienvenue a
Wilkommen in
Velkommen til   Hull

Linked with

Freetown (Sierra Leone)
Raleigh (USA)
Rotterdam (Netherlands)
Reykjavik (Iceland)

But that is not all. There follows a long series of symbols indicating the pleasures that lie ahead. Or could they be Japanese for Welcome? The visitor has no idea, as he has driven past the signboard along a fast dual carriageway, and has only had time to read the first line. Unless, that is, he has arrived on foot or on horseback, and I doubt whether many visitors to Hull do that nowadays.

Fortunately, you and I already know that Hull is not Hull. It is Kingston.

We also know that Hull, as distinct from Thames, is the name of the river on which Kingston stands. Unlike the Thames, the Hull is a bare five leagues in length, with nothing else standing upon it other than coarse fishermen.

But not everyone is aware of these subtleties of identity, which were devised long ago by the city's founding fathers in search of a word of more than four letters with which to fill their roadside sign.

In consequence, on arriving at the reception desk of the hotel in which he will be speaking, the speaker has to wait for the confused visitor in front to be attended to, and cannot help overhearing the conversation. The visitor may well have come from Freetown, Raleigh, Rotterdam or Reykjavik.

'Excuse me,' says the visitor to the man behind the desk, 'Vere iss Ull?'

'I beg you pardon, sir?'

'Vere – is – Ull?'

'Er . . . will you write it down for me please, sir?'

The visitor writes it down: H U L L

'Ah!' says the receptionist. 'You are in Hull.'

'Vot you say?'

'YOU – ARE – IN – HULL'

'But no. I am in KEENGSTON.'

'No sir, THIS IS HULL.'

'But se sign says 'K-I-N-G-S-T-O-N!'

'No, Sir, this is Hull, and you are in the right city.'

'Zis I cannot understand. Can you tell me, vere is ze Station Hotel, Hull?'

'This is the Station Hotel, Hull, sir.'

'But ze sign say *Royal* Hotel!'

'This is the Royal Hotel, sir.'

'But I am booked into ze *Station* Hotel!'

'This is often still called the Station Hotel, sir, but it is now the Royal Hotel.'

At last the visitor has established that he is in the right city, and the right hotel. He signs in, is given his room key, and hastens off to his room. The speaker, in no doubt as to his whereabouts, also signs in and hastens to his room. On the fifth floor he passes the same visitor hastening back again, presumably having discovered that he is on the wrong floor of the right hotel in the right city.

The speaker finds his room, unlocks the door and enters, only to find two people already in it. They are workmen with blowtorches, and the room has no floorboards. The speaker hastens back to the reception desk, to find the visitor in front of him, again in conversation with the receptionist.

'Zere is already somevon else in my room!' he protests.

'And in mine, and mine has no floorboards,' interjects the speaker.

Eventually, a profusely apologetic receptionist finds alternative rooms, and the confused visitor spends, we hope, a more comfortable night than the speaker, who has been redirected to a room the size of a Victorian wardrobe.

Not long after that occurrence, the hotel was burnt to the ground.

But although one source of mistaken identity has thus been tidied-up, the Kingston-upon/or-Hull problem is still with us. I would not wish to suggest however that we be delivered from it by similar means.

Johnson's Yard, Thirsk

This is but one of many old yards in the town centre:
the building on the right forms the back room of
a butcher's shop. I have only once been able to speak in
the centre of Thirsk (and not in the butcher's shop). On
the other occasions I have found myself, like the railway
station, diverted well outside the town. Apart from a certain
veterinary practice, Thirsk also sustains a thriving Rotary
Club and, yes, the Inner Wheel.

 **is for ILLUMINATION (Unwanted)**

Stray light is what the speaker with slides does not want.

During daylight hours it filters in remorselessly through ill-fitting, torn or misshapen curtains, which resist all efforts to make ends meet, or worse. On one occasion, mine was the first attempt to black out a hall the day after curtains had been newly-fitted by a hard-working volunteer. The lot fell to the floor, fittings and all, one after the other.

It is for this reason that I try to avoid engagements during the summer months – say, between May and early September. Even during the British summer, the sun can effectively neutralize what one is trying to do. Neverthless, the importance of the occasion, and the enthusiasm of one's hosts, must sometimes prevail.

So it was one summer's evening that I set out to the annual dinner of members of an Inner Wheel club, near to an attractive market-town well-known for its literary and veterinary connections.

For those who may not know, the Inner Wheel is one of a number of related organizations enjoying geometrical, mechanical and circulatory titles and emblems. I refer (in reverse alphabetical order rather than in any order of rectitude) to those pillars of social and communal respectability: Tangent, Round Table, Rotaract, Rotary, Ladies' Circle and tonight's hostesses, Inner Wheel.

Members of Inner Wheel are the wives of Rotarians. They organize their own functions and activities. In addition they are required by their husbands, who have more important things to do, to provide full service back-up for their husbands' functions and activities. Hence the title Inner Wheel, which their husbands recognize as conveying an appropriate sense of hard-working activity within a more gently revolving, but more significant, whole.

Let us now enter into the spirit of an occasion organized by the Inner Wheel, for once, for their own enjoyment.

This evening's event is held in the dining room of the national headquarters of a men's outfitters of distinction. As you would expect, this is a spacious, tasteful and well-appointed room in which to dine. It is normally used only during the day, and its extensive windows are therefore uncurtained, to allow uninter-rupted and attractive views of the hills beyond. They face west.

As we enter the room, we are bathed in brilliant evening sunshine. It continues to bless us with its light as we dine, and as we take our coffee, and as we mix in convivial conversation afterwards. It hangs there in the sky as we continue with our convivial conversation, waiting for it to set, for my talk should have started half-an-hour ago. But still it is there, now a red orb, until finally it sinks behind the purple hills at ten o'clock, and at last we can start.

Tonight the Inner Wheel will be rotating homewards rather later than usual. It will not arrive home until long after the hour at which good Rotarians, having conscientiously transferred their Rotary badges to their pyjama lapels, have settled down for the night.

During the winter season the main difficulty is not so much to keep out the daylight, as to combat artificial light from elsewhere. Usually it obtrudes through swing doors with glass windows, which are commonly wedged open to ventilate the kitchen; or similar doors to the bar, where the rest of the world is getting on with its life, noisily.

But not only will the speaker-with-slides have to contend with extraneous light: his real difficulties are about the begin. After an introductory chat for a minute or two with the room-lights on, he will ask for darkness so that the show can start.

For some time, nothing happens. Then some of the lights begin to go out, one by one. But one light in the front left-hand corner will not go out.

Helpful members of the audience rise noisily from their chairs and wander about, trying switches that they believe no one else has tried. Several lights go on again. More members of the audience get up and join in the hunt. In trying to find switches, I have known men break into the head porter's office, or to put up ladders and climb into the rafters.

Suddenly the room is plunged into darkness. There are sounds of confusion as the helpful members of the audience try to regain their seats, without success. The speaker, having earlier been standing ready at his controls, has wandered from them, and has no idea where to find the switch for the projector. Nor can he find the torch that he has carefully positioned for just such a contingency. So the lights have to go on again until at last the audience is seated and the speaker is in control.

Finally, the lights are out.

Except the one in the front left-hand corner.

Merchant Taylors' Hall, York

The scene of diverse and enjoyable convivial occasions! York has more than its share of Ancient Institutions, including not only the Merchant Taylors, but also the Merchant Adventurers and the Gilds of Cordwainers, Builders and the like. Each Company has its own ancient, timbered hall, dating back to the 14th Century. Their members, whilst pursuing entirely respectable professions, do not necessarily ply the trade of their title. There are also the Freemen of York, who now admit Freewomen. They have no Hall to go to, but they do have the right to graze their goats on York's pastures.

 **is for JERUSALEM**

As a small boy I used to wonder what had happened to the beginning of the opening sentence of Jerusalem, before the AND. What words had been missed out, and why shouldn't we sing them?

But as one grows older, one realizes that what the opening of Jerusalem lacks in words, it more than makes up for in the splendour, complexity and difficulty of execution of its piano introduction:

There is something peremptory about the **'AND'**. Whoever uses it to start his question expects no satisfactory answer, e.g.: 'And why have you come in with dirty knees, boy?' Try leaving the 'And' off the beginning of Jerusalem, and you'll see what I mean.

Did you know, by the way, that there are no less than six hymns in *Hymns Ancient and Modern* and *Songs of Praise* beginning with 'And'? They all use the word as a verbal dig in the ribs for inattentive members of the congregation. Yet for sheer compelling majesty, Jerusalem leaves the others far behind.

What has all this to do with the speaker? Everything.

Any speaker worth his salt has spoken to members of the National Federation of Women's Institutes, whether at Institute level, group level or at some level yet more exalted. Jerusalem is their inspirational hymn, and is usually sung at the beginning of a meeting, before business starts. The quality of performance varies in degree of excellence, governed largely by the state of the piano and the ability of the pianist to surmount the demands of the introduction, accompaniment and ending.

The speaker is usually in a position to assess the performance, as he is still preparing his equipment on the stage when the pianist, probably close beside him, suddenly strikes the first chord. The speaker hurriedly assumes an appropriately respectful stance as the hymn is sung, by all, word-perfect, throughout both verses. He is in full view of those who are singing, and has therefore made sure that he knows the words.

Without a hymn-book to absorb his attention, he is at first at a loss as to where to look while singing: straight ahead, at the ceiling, at the floor, or at the well-polished shoes of the ladies on the front row.

But then he realizes that he can comfortably look everyone else in the eye. For while they are singing, the ladies look only at the floor or the ceiling. It is only when England's green and pleasant land has been attained for the second time round that their collective gaze switches suddenly to one recipient: the pianist. They are willing her on in her battle with the concluding, stirring chords:

It is noticeable that there is a certain variation in the degree of enthusiasm with which Jerusalem is sung, as between one group and another. Recently I heard a president open the meeting by announcing:

'Good evening ladies. Tonight we are not going to have Jerusalem . . .'

A fluttering of discreet relief was detectable among the members, but was cut short as the president continued:

'. . . until the visitors arrive.'

Some time later the late-arriving visitors from other institutes did arrive, clearly believing that quite inadvertently they had missed the singing of Jerusalem. But they were not to be thus disappointed. Not only was it sung; but its performance and accompaniment excelled any other that I have heard for sheer musicianship and accuracy.

By contrast, I recall an evening when I was trying to set up my gear on a somewhat cramped stage, much of which was occupied by a large, upright piano. I asked one of the members – the treasurer, I think – whether I could move the piano out of the way.

'I'm afraid it'll be needed', she said, beginning to remove from it the tailored green cover which carefully protected it.

The president hurried towards us.

'For goodness' sake put that cover back on again,' she said, seizing it, 'before Margaret arrives!'

I did not learn who Margaret was, nor did we have Jerusalem.

Turning now to the music of the institutes beyond the borders of England's pleasant pastures green, I have to confess that I have never had the pleasure of speaking at a meeting of the Welsh WI, nor of the Scottish equivalent, the Scottish Women's Rural Institutes.

The Welsh WI members, I understand, unfailingly sing *Hen wlad fy nhadau* (Land of My Fathers), and I have no doubt that they sing it with the same verve, conviction and harmony, if not the volume, as their compatriots before a match at Cardiff Arms Park.

On the other hand the Scottish women, I am informed, enjoy a wide choice of permissible songs of a rousing nature. Here is but one example, sung to the tune *Sound the Pibroch:*

VERSE 1:   *North and South and East and West,*
                          Highlands, Lowlands, home is best,
                          Learn the watch-word on each breast
                          All for home and country.

CHORUS: *Tha tighin fodham, fodham, fodham,*
                          Tha tighin fodham, fodham, eirigh
                          Tha tighin fodham, fodham, fodham,
                          All for home and country

VERSES 2, 3, 4 and 5, each with CHORUS, follow.

It is thus evident that the Scottish and the Welsh women preface their meetings with songs in praise of their nations' achievements. It is left to the English to express, in song, their determination to introduce someone else's.

In conclusion, stepping now out of the rural territory of the WI and into the confines of the Town, I was interested to note a subtle change in orientation when I had the pleasure of visiting a certain branch of the Townswomen's Guild.

The proud and well-measured words of their opening song, written by one of their own members, are artistically inscribed on a scroll held aloft by the chairman so that the guest speaker can read them. I cannot remember the words, but I do recall that they are sung to the tune Austria, elsewhere recognized as the German national anthem.

A nice balance is later achieved, however, with the singing of God Save the Queen, after which all go home.

St. Cuthbert's, Darlington

Though it has played an historic role in the development of our railways, Darlington remains essentially a country town, with its own thriving culture and many active organisations. St. Cuthbert's Church is in the heart of the town, yet its grounds provide a quiet and welcome retreat from the nearby swirling traffic. The St. Cuthbert's Centre, within the grounds, is a well-appointed, modern meeting place, in which can be found the longest curtain draw-cords that I have yet encountered.

75

 **is for KEY**

As we saw under CHAIRMAN, if you do not have a key, you may not be able to get out. More importantly perhaps, a key is also what you need to get in.

I had arrived a little earlier than arranged, outside the large hall of a large church, for a fund-raising event in aid of its large organ fund. It was no surprise to find that no one else had arrived, so I unloaded the car and piled my equipment outside the door of the hall, which was locked.

Still no one else had arrived. I decided to check the date on a nearby noticeboard, which was just discernible in the darkness. By the light of my torch I read, not a poster about my talk, but the words:

WHATEVER *SEEMS* EVIL
IS EVIL

Beyond the wayside pulpit I tracked down the noticeboard, which was positioned to provide a logical afterthought to this doom-laden message. It bore my name, the correct date, and the correct time of 7.30pm.

At last members of the paying public were beginning to arrive. The door remained locked, and a member of the committee set off on foot into the night to find whoever had the key.

A queue had now developed in the street, and the key still had not arrived. Another member of the committee stepped forward. He had thought of someone else who might have the key, and set off into the night on his bicycle.

By now an entire audience of some 200 people had assembled, waiting patiently (for most were dedicated members of the congregation) to be let in. Little did they know that even when the door was opened, if ever, I would need half-an-hour's preparation before the show could start. It was the first time I'd had to queue to hear myself speak.

77

'I'd better go and see where they've got to,' said a third member of the committee and drove off into the night in his car.

At that moment a fourth person, who had not been with us earlier, arrived.

'You're all in good time!' he said cheerfully.

'What d'you mean?' said the man behind me. 'Can't you read the notice?'

'Oh I don't know anything about Evil – I've come to open the doors for that talk at eight o'clock', replied the man with the key, carrying out his mission before he disappeared whence he had come. The queue filed in, thankful that their wait was at an end, and too forgiving to complain that the doorman had got the time wrong.

Half an hour later the organ fund event at last began.

I do not know whether the three searchers who had gone off into the night on foot, awheel and by car, ever returned. But the key had arrived, and Whatever Seemed Evil had won the day for the organ.

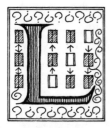 **is for LIFT**

Of all the varying venues in which the speaker is likely to find himself, only a few will have a lift. This is unfortunate bearing in mind the universal Law of Unequal Levels, which dictates that wherever in the building you are required to speak, it will not be at the level at which you happen to be at the time (see OBSTACLE).

Lifts are sometimes found in:

a Hotels, for the use of porters
b Civic establishments, for the use of civic figures
c Hospitals, for the use of unconscious patients

Lifts are never found in:

a Village halls
b Church halls
c Memorial halls
d Listed buildings
e Unlisted buildings

That is, in the places in which you are most likely to be required to speak.

If you are fortunate enough to find that your venue has a lift, do not attempt to use it unless the lift-cage is spacious enough to allow you to:

a Enter with your equipment
b Secure the equipment with one hand while operating the lift buttons with the other

    c Avoid getting your elbow trapped in the lift doors

    d Avoid standing, or positioning your equipment, on the feet of five prospective members of your audience, who have attempted to enter the lift cage with you

    e Get out at the requisite floor before the lift, of its own accord, returns to earth

Failing any of these requirements (and I have known them all fail at once), you will have to take to the stairs.

Perhaps my most challenging lift experience occurred in a Victorian hotel, with a magnificent ballroom in which I was to speak. It was not quite old enough to be a listed building, but much too old to have been designed with a lift. As a gesture to technology, a lift had much later been added as an afterthought, to occupy a space originally designed for one Victorian potted plant.

Wheeling my equipment-laden sack-barrow before me, I approached the lift and pressed the call-button. After some time the doors slid open, and out walked a porter, bent on more important business than mine. The porter looked considerably larger than the space he had vacated.

I pushed the sack-barrow towards the back of the lift, but the topmost item of the load (which was also the widest) became trapped in the doors. I could move neither in nor out. Eventually I managed to reach inside, and by pressing every unseen button in turn, found the Door Open button. I was just in time to haul out my possessions before the doors slammed shut, and the lift went empty and unseen on its way. I was back to square one, as they say.

I pressed the call-button again. Again the lift doors slid open, and out walked *the same porter*, still on more important business than mine. There was no time to wonder how or why be came to be there a second time. I thrust myself and my load into the lift, and again the doors closed. Again they clamped firmly on to my widest item, the process was repeated, and again I had to beat a retreat. I was getting nowhere.

I pressed the call-button for one last try. After a short time the lift doors opened. Out came, not the porter, but the attractive receptionist who had wished me good morning as I had entered the hotel. There was no time to wonder how she got there. For like the porter, she had more important business than mine, and clearly had neither time nor wish to be trapped in the lift with me.

The time had come for desperate measures. With the receptionist gone, I thrust the sack-barrow into the lift, then rushed out of it before the doors closed. While my load journeyed upwards, I raced up the stairs to the second floor, and was just in time to receive and retrieve the lift's contents. My expectant hostess, unaware of the interfloor drama that had been taking place, greeted me.

'Ah,' she exclaimed, 'we wondered where you were! We called the porter to look for you. He said he'd searched every floor, but you seemed to have disappeared!'

Afterwards, out of curiosity, I measured with hand-spans the size of the lift. It was twenty-nine inches square from wall to wall, with a door-opening twenty-four inches wide. No doubt it was made-to-measure for the porter. But it was no match for my needs.

All I ask is a lift with space enough for me, my ten bits of equipment, and maybe the receptionist. Not the porter.

The Spa Hotel, Ripon

On the Eleventh Day of Christmas, the Ripon Women's Luncheon Club did not have their eleven pipers piping. They had to put up with me instead, and the Christmas decorations were coming down even as I spoke. But they could not have chosen to meet in a more splendid hostelry (revisited here in summer), with its expansive lawns and gardens, gracious trees, and somewhere, I suppose, a health-bestowing spring.

 **is also for LUNCHEON MEETING**

If you thought that we had finished with this subject under 'HANDBAG', I am happy to say that we have not. We then dealt only with the preliminaries. Now for the substance.

For the speaker, a luncheon meeting usually presents a special challenge, because more often than not the lunchers lunch in the same room as that in which the speaker speaks.

For those gifted speakers who require no visible means of support in the form of slides, this is no hindrance: they simply wait until everyone has lunched, then stand up and speak – all accomplished in the space of a square foot or two.

As for the rest of us, we have problems. Long before the formalities begin, we have to prepare to set up our equipment. This entails a detailed reconnaissance of the room, its surrounds, the fittings, the staff, and the early arrivals among the membership (see HANDBAG).

It is therefore usually necessary to set off from home not long after breakfast, in order to arrive round about morning coffee-time. The next hour or so is spent in assessing, forming and implementing one's plan of action, including the careful positioning of all equipment and the laying of cables and wires thereto. When all is prepared, the under-manager walks in, and takes one look.

'You're not going to need these . . . er . . . *things* here during lunch, are you, sir?' he asks, courteously but firmly.

His statement (for such is the nature of his question) is not unfamiliar. He takes me through my offences:

1. My projector-stand and projector will be in the way of the serving staff as they toil to serve 120 luncheons.
2. My loudspeakers are occupying the tables that will be required for 120 coffee-cups.
3. The table from which I will operate is blocking the emergency fire exit.
4. My screen will impede 120 luncheon club members as they arrive from the bar.
5. My wires will trip up the serving staff and everyone else.
6. I AM IN BREACH OF THE HEALTH AND SAFETY AT WORK ACT.

'Would you mind moving these things out of the way, sir?'
This is an order, not a request. I try to carry it out with good grace.

Now I must prepare my Plan B, which will entail moving everything back into place after the serving staff have finished serving coffee. That will be in another two hours' time.

But before it can be implemented, I am able to put aside such considerations, for I have been invited to join the president and her friends in the comfortable armchairs of the lounge bar. For the next half-hour I enjoy the lively conviviality of their company. The president and I are in the middle of an interesting conversation, when the under-manager, eyeing me with suspicion, announces in ringing tones that the luncheon is about to be served. I rise instinctively at his bidding, but find myself being asked to continue to be seated.

In some luncheon clubs, the members simply drift in any order into the dining room, and sit down.

In others – as on this occasion – something completely different happens. Upon the luncheon announcement, the members at large proceed into the dining room, but remain standing silently at their places (ordained by whatever means has triumphed: See HANDBAG). The president, remaining seated in the lounge bar, continues to converse interestingly with the speaker, also seated.

After a seemly period – judged I believe by the president to be the longest that members will stand for – she brings the conversation elegantly to an end, leads the speaker into the dining room, and proceeds round the room towards the top table, which is as far away as possible from the door of entry.

The members continue to stand silently. What is the speaker to do? March silently ahead, looking neither to left nor right? Attempt to resume unconcernedly the conversation with the president that began in the bar? Wave cheerful greetings to the members *en route*?

Having failed to solve this problem myself, I cannot offer advice. In some respects it would help if members broke into the singing of Jerusalem; but this is a luncheon club, not one of your unseemly evening knees-ups. Silence therefore prevails, broken only by the distant voice of the under-manager behind the swing doors to the kitchen, briefing his staff to have no truck with the speaker and his equipment.

When at last the president and speaker have arrived at their places at the top table, the president says grace. Unlike the unchanging grace with which luncheoning men are apt to invoke blessing upon their proceedings, this grace has been personally and appropriately chosen for today. At last, all are seated and luncheon commences.

The speaker takes a special interest in the speed of service, not because he cannot wait for his vol-au-vents, but because every quarter-hour added to the service-time is a quarter-of-an-hour off his speaking-time. The temperature of the vegetable-salvers is a useful indicator of what can be expected. As a rule-of-thumb, the colder the dish, the slower will be the service, and the less the speaker will be expected to say when his time comes. Conversely, hotter dishes usually portend faster service, and a longer stint ahead for the speaker.

Not so long ago, I was applying this test to the salver containing the roast potatoes. I should have taken warning from the heavy serving-napkin used by the waitress (though that of itself can mean nothing: the colder the contents, the greater can be the insulation). Unprepared as I was, I would swear that I heard the sound of my own finger-tips sizzling.

My cry of agony must have been heard on the hill-tops surrounding the town. As I wrung my hand, a sudden silence descended on the dining room. Someone cried 'Dip it in water!'. The president, with great presence of mind, thrust my fingertips into her glass of, as I recall, white wine. Thus was I able to complete my meal, which was served like lightning, and a full stint was later served by the speaker.

But the luncheon is usually less eventful, and the speaker can readily forget why he is here. He is abruptly reminded by the announcement of the Loyal Toast, secured by a sharp blow of the president's gavel on her block (though I have known a president shatter her side-plate by mistake). He remembers that now is the time for him to spring into action with positioning his equipment. Fortunately he no longer needs to concern himself with the Health and Safety at Work Act, as all the people at work have gone.

For what may happen next, see PROJECTOR and REMOTE CONTROL.

But let us now take it that we are in mid-afternoon, and the lunching and the speaking are over. The members retire, informally now, to the lounge for a relaxed cup of afternoon tea. They have of course invited the speaker to join them, and he is glad to postpone the packing-up of his equipment as long as he can.

Perhaps an hour later, having enjoyed imbibing, talking, lunching, speaking and tea-drinking with the hospitable ladies of the luncheon club, the speaker drives home into the sunset, content with having done an enjoyable lunchtime's work.

On arriving home as the shadows fall, his wife asks him where he's been all day, and how he got his fingers burnt.

Royal Baths and Assembly Rooms, Harrogate

Not to be outdone by lesser creations to the south, this imposing edifice, built in 1897, combines at one fell swoop all you ever needed to know about the Albert Hall, Westminster Abbey and Buckingham Palace. True, Royalty didn't actually reside here, but they took its waters, and its acoustics are unmistakably those of the Royal Bathroom.

 **is for MICROPHONE**

The Lord never intended us to use the microphone.

Normally I avoid its use. In all but the worst of acoustics or the largest of auditoriums, the unamplified human voice, provided that it's loud and clear, is more easily heard than a disembodied noise coming out of a loudspeaker.

When I first became involved in these talks, I was told: 'Always speak to the people on the back row, so that they can hear every word you say.' I try to do this, but it does seem hard luck on those on the front row, who often have to sit very near to me indeed.

It is a well-known phenomenon that people never willingly sit on the front row anywhere, for anything. Unless, that is, they are religious or political activists, in which case my talks would provide them with only sparse fare. In my audiences, people sit on the front row solely because they arrive too late to sit at the back. No one sitting on the front row has ever actually compla ned that I am speaking to the people at the back and not to them; but that is only because I have numbed their senses.

Acoustics can vary greatly. They range from the most ringing that I have ever encountered (in the lovely parish church in Patterdale) to the most intimate (in a bookshop, in which the 100-strong unfortunate customers had to be arranged on the bookshelves).

Most acoustically interesting of all, in my experience, was one of the spacious halls of the Royal Baths, Harrogate, under a magnificent glass dome. I was reminded of Bing Crosby's contribution to my cultural upbringing:

Oh, you blow that horn
An' the music goes round and round
Oh-ho-ho-ho,
Ho-ho
An' it comes out
Here

Unlike the music of Bing Crosby's horn, my voice didn't come out here, or anywhere else. It disappeared into the roof, and never came down again.

The audience, as it happened, were members of a certain highly respectable non-activist tea-club in search only of enjoyment. In the absence of an audible commentary, I am sure that they would have found much greater enjoyment from any 78 RPM gramophone record played at home.

Sometimes, however, because of the nature of the hall or the polite insistence of your hosts, or both, you have to use the microphone. This means that you surrender authority to an unseen hand operating the volume controls, or to an even more unseen Automatic Sound Sensor.

If you speak too loudly, or face the wrong way, or stand near a loudspeaker, the audience can be made to suffer from an ear-piercing whistle or howl known as positive feedback. This well-known ploy is sometimes called upon to secure attention during after-lunch sessions. For the same purpose, I also find it useful on occasions suddenly to turn up to full volume the sound of the full peal of the bells of York Minster.

You may come across three types of microphone:

First, the **stand microphone.** This slides up and down according to whether it is being used by the chairman, the secretary or the speaker. It must be in front of your face, and your face may not therefore move. It is never at the right height for whoever is using it. Whenever it is slid up and down, it causes thunderous rumblings. It can usually be detached from the stand, often unintentionally, causing louder and more intensive sounds.

Second, the **clip-on microphone.** This tiny device clips on to your tie or lapel or some other handy concealment near to where your voice belongs. Cleverly, it picks up your words before they have passed your lips, by eavesdropping through your rib-cage. The audience is therefore always one syllable ahead of you. Moreover, you are tethered by the lead to your speaking-post, like a goat to its grazing ground. If you forgetfully wander beyond the length of your tether, which is usually about three feet, you are either jerked to a halt, or your tie is torn and your words wasted.

Most ingenious of all is the **transmitter microphone.** It is similar to the clip-on, except that instead of a tether you have a second device in your pocket. This transmits what you are saying to a receiver somewhere-or-other – maybe the odd passing satellite – and your voice fills the hall after circling the earth. Sadly, it's easy to forget that you have on your person a switched-on transmitter microphone, and the world continues to listen to your every word long after you thought you had finished publicly speaking.

The Lord never intended us to use The Microphone.

 **is for NECKWEAR**

The speaker tries to wear what he believes the audience expects, though he is seldom told. But as we have seen earlier, the Hull Literary and Philosophical Society spells out its requirements in meticulous detail, including the rule that the speaker shall wear formal dress.

As I was to discover, these rules are characteristic of the excellence and thoroughness of the organization of the Society, which can in no way be blamed for my discomfiture when I had the privilege of speaking to them (or rather lecturing, as their rules require).

Let us now turn to neckwear.

On hearing that I was to wear formal dress for the society, my wife persuaded me that it was high time I bought myself a new dress shirt, to replace the one that I had known, worn and loved since my student days. So I set off in search of a dress shirt that would be in keeping with the final decade of the twentieth century, not to mention the first two decades of the twenty-first.

The assistant in the menswear store explained to me that the smart formal man of the 1990s wears not a turn-down collar, but a wing-collar, as was fashionable in the 1890s. Gratefully I accepted his advice and bought such a shirt. But then a thought struck me: with no turn-down collar, would not the hollow sham of my elasticated bow-tie (also from student days) be revealed for all to see? I sought reassurance from the assistant.

To digress: I must here confess that I have never been able to tie a real bow-tie. I have always envied a friend who, in the course of the students' play production in which we had parts, was required to tie his bow tie on-stage while speaking his lines. After many a tutorial he became tie-perfect as well as word-perfect. Forty years on, he still retains the gift of tying a bow tie – but only by simultaneously reciting his lines from the play, which happened to be *'The Flashing Stream*, by Charles Morgan.

My only extraneous role in that production was to play the piano behind the scenes, and I have therefore gone through life with a false bow-tie.

'Never mind, sir,' said the shop assistant, 'it won't show.' I accepted his advice, and took the shirt home with no further thought, other than basking in the unaccustomed praise of our sons when my wife told them that I had at last moved into the 1990s.

To return to my evening with the Hull Lit and Phil: In addition to all other aspects of four-star provision, the society had arranged overnight accommodation for the speaker in the four-star hotel in which it met (since, alas, consumed by fire). I had found my room, and had nearly finished changing into the requisite formal dress, complete with 1990s wing-collar shirt. All that remained was the bow-tie – a quick hook-and-eye job with the elastic, and that would be that.

But then I discovered that the shop assistant had been economical with the truth. The falsity of my bow-tie was only too obvious: where there should have been a dignified fold of black velvet, a thin bit of elastic and its metal connections were prominently framed under my left ear, starkly revealed by the non-turned-down 1990-style wing-collar.

The City of Kingston upon Hull at 7.20pm on a wet winter's night is not the place to go in search of a real bow-tie, nor tuition in the tying thereof. The impossibility is compounded when in five minutes' time one is due to be formally escorted onto the podium of a resplendent auditorium where, already waiting in their seats, are 350 members of a Literary and Philosophical Society.

I could only hope that my ceremonial entry would be from stage left, so that the falsity of my tie could be concealed until I could call for darkness. It was not. We entered not only from stage right, but also along most of the right flank of the audience. My bit of elastic was remorselessly exposed, and with it my flagrant breach of the society's requirement of authentic formal dress. I expected to be politely but firmly ejected.

But the Society turned out to be as magnanimous as it was philosophical. Not only was I allowed to remain, but the projection, screen and acoustics (there is a rule requiring the use of a microphone) were of the highest standard I have found anywhere. Moreover, I enjoyed my first opportunity to use a laser-pointer, with which the speaker was equipped by the Society (see POINTER).

The evening was rounded off with an excellent dinner party with the president, the council and his personal guests (all in authentic formal dress). The Note for Lecturers states: 'The dinner is not unduly prolonged, and the lecturer can expect to retire to bed at a reasonable hour.' I am not sure that this rule was meticulously observed: an excellent evening continued well into the night, in the course of which the correctness of neckwear came to matter little.

That should have been the end of this lengthy dissertation on NECKWEAR, but there is a corollary of which you should be aware.

After my experience with the Hull Lit and Phil, it was clear that I would have to buy a new tie, suitable for my 1990s wing-collar. I walked into the nearest branch of Moss Bros, confident that they would have the answer. Sure enough, in no time at all I was fixed up with a 1990s false bow-tie, suitable for a 1990s collar. This time I was not going to be foolish enough to leave it until five minutes before my next public appearance. As soon as I got home, I tried on my new, non-elasticated, 1990s tie.

There seemed to be rather a lot of it. It went not once, but twice round my neck.

After fruitless attempts at adjustment, I accepted at last that the tie was not meant for me, and returned to Moss Bros to change it.

As I entered the Moss Bros shop, the sign on the glass swing-doors caught my eye. I had earlier taken it to be a new and imposing Moss Bros marketing slogan:

HIGH AND MIGHTY, it said.

I stepped back and surveyed the shop-fronts, particularly the one next door.

MOSS BROS, it said.

So my transaction had not been with Moss Bros at all, but with a highly-specialized and totally unconnected men's outfitter, with the two inconsiderately located cheek by jowl.

I now know that HIGH AND MIGHTY caters solely for men who are of spectacular height, or girth, or both. I hope against hope that I shall not need to visit them again.

☆　　☆　　☆

 **is for OBSTACLE**

We concern ourselves here with a routine test of physique and subterfuge confronting the speaker: how to get himself and his equipment into the place in which he is expected to speak. The place may be a room, a hall, a theatre, or even more grandly an auditorium. But whatever its pretensions, it is sure to present an obstacle course, as any speaker will quickly discover.

My equipment happens to consist of ten items, of various shapes and sizes. In total they weigh about 200lbs, which is about the weight of one-and-three-quarter sacks of coal. Not that I carry my things around in coal sacks: they are in separate bits and pieces, shaped mostly by the designers of hi-fi and projection equipment, and never intended to be carried anywhere.

To shift these things to and from my car I use a special mode of transport: a platform with a ledge and a pair of wheels at one end, and handles at the other. Some people would call it a *luggage-wheels*; but this induces an immediate conflict between singular and plural, and there is already enough conflict around. I must therefore call a spade a spade, and stick to my SACK-BARROW – redolent though it is of agricultural heavy labour among potato mountains, and unbecoming of the aspiring elegant speaker.

As you now know, my equipment requires two journeys of the sack-barrow. In addition there is a six-foot folded screen. Because of its excessive length it cannot be persuaded to fit on the sack-barrow. It must instead be borne ahead by hand on its own, vertically or horizontally or at whatever angle it may assume of its own accord, to the danger of yourself and any unwise bystanders.

☆　　☆　　☆

So much for my own load. You may have more, or you may have less. But whatever may be the case, the first deterrent to your progress is likely to be the fire regulations.

The fire regulations require that EVERY ENTRANCE DOOR:

1 Shall be capable of opening only towards, that is against, you

2 Shall be held firmly shut by a powerful return-spring

3 Shall resist your every effort to open it with one hand while trying to control and propel your sackbarrow with the other

4 Shall be too narrow to allow your load to pass through without opening the door's twin, which shall be firmly secured with inset bolts top and bottom, which no one has been able to shift since last Christmas

The first obstacle is therefore the ADVERSELY SWINGING DOOR. This can be surmounted only by a specialised technique, requiring the use of hands, elbows, shoulders, knees, feet and head, and the harder the head, the better.

An alternative obstacle is the REVOLVING DOOR. This is to be found obstructing the entrance to establishments such as Hotels and Baths, with names often starting with the word Royal. They were never intended to be entered by people with sack-barrows, and we must therefore consider them in more detail.

Even if you manage to enter a revolving door with a laden sack-barrow, you will never get out again. Wedged by the wheels in front and your heels behind, you are unable to progress forward or backward. Your only hope is that a guest trapped in the opposite half of the revolving door will desperately generate enough momentum to propel you round, in two-inch-jerks. But the moment you come round to the inner sanctum, you must jump for it. Otherwise, the next incomer will propel you round and outwards again, *ad infinitum.*

There are two means of evading the revolving door trap. The first is to transform it into a passageway, by folding it back on itself. Unfortunately this can be effected only by the doorman, whose presence and willingness cannot be counted upon. The alternative is to abandon the sack-barrow altogether, and to carry each item round, through and beyond, time after time after time. Unless, that is, you are entering our Tesco superstore, whose vast revolving door would accommodate a tractor. But I have not yet been invited to speak in a Tesco superstore.

Assuming that you have contrived to overcome the obstacle of the entrance doors, you must concern yourself next with the Law of Unequal Levels.

This law prescribes that the world in which you will be speaking will never be at the same level as the world outside. You will therefore have to get yourself and your sack-barrow up (or down) as many steps and staircases as may be necessary to attain the right altitude (or depth, as the case may be).

Occasionally you may find a lift. We have already dealt with this at some length (see LIFT). Let us assume, realistically, that you have acknowledged defeat by the lift, and must therefore take to the stairs.

You may be surprised to know that a sack-barrow and its load can, with certain exceptions, climb steps and whole flights of stairs.

All you have to do is provide the motive power, thus:

● Take a firm grip on the handles and approach the staircase backwards. Climb the stairs backwards until your arms are fully extended, then pull hard. The wheels of the sack-barrow will slowly climb the bottom step vertically, then very suddenly horizontally. At this moment it is imperative to keep your balance. On no account sit down or be drawn forward, or you will return rapidly whence you came.

- Repeat this process as often as is necessary, until you fall backwards on arriving unexpectedly at the top step. Pick yourself up with your belongings, take them to their destination and return for the next load.

- To descend a staircase with a loaded sack-barrow, adopt the same posture as above, but strive to lower the wheels gently from one step to the next. You will not succeed in this objective, but with care you may prevent your descent from running altogether out of control. It is a good idea to ensure beforehand if you can that no one else is on the stairs at the time.

I have used this technique to ascend and descend a great many flights of steps and stairs. Assuming a modest average of only ten upward steps per speaking engagement, my sack-barrow and I have in the course of time ascended and descended at least two thousand feet.

Occasionally one experiences the sensation of taking off into space.

This was vividly demonstrated one March night when I arrived to speak in the village of Fearby-with-Healey, in one of the remoter Yorkshire Dales. A north-westerly gale howled down the valley, funnelling straight off the moors, driving before it sheets of horizontal rain. The rain in turn funnelled into a torrent down the village street or, rather, the steep lane which joins Fearby at one end with Healey at the other, about a mile apart.

I was searching for the village hall. Half-way between the two villages, my headlights picked out, rising out of the torrent, a white wicket-gate and hand-rails. It was at least a sign of

The Village Hall, Fearby:
Two Impressions

Some time after the experience described opposite,
I returned to discover the real Fearby. Gone was
the horizontal rain. On this mellow September
afternoon, the only sound to disturb the sunlit
quietness was the cooing of doves.

civilization, though no village hall was visible. In the light of my torch, I could see only a steep flight of concrete steps, disappearing upwards into the howling, swirling darkness.

Disbelievingly, I set off on this ascent into the unknown. For all I could discern, it might have been the weather-lashed summit of some remote Scottish peak. But at last, at the top of the ascent, I found the village hall of Fearby-with-Healey, along with the indomitable members of the Women's Institutes of Fearby, Healey and others of the greater Group of Skelldale.

Never has my sack-barrow so nearly taken-off as on that ascent, buffeted by the roaring storm, which subsequently threatened to blow the roof of the village hall all the way from Healey to Fearby. But the warmth of the welcome within was as unabated as the storm without.

Two forms of staircase are unassailable by sack-barrow, and you might as well not even try.

The first is the spiral staircase. Although well-suited to the climbing of church towers, it is quite unsuitable for the barrowing of sacks or anything else. As I have discovered, a sack-barrow will overturn on the first sharply-angled step. Only two or three such steps in an otherwise straight flight are enough to defeat you.

We come finally to staircases often found in buildings of Victorian origin: I refer to stairs with Projecting Lips. The sack-barrow is stopped in its tracks. This is due not to anatomical attraction, but to the trapping effect that the projecting edges have on the wheels. The lips make upward progress totally impossible, and you will have to carry your equipment upstairs piecemeal.

The most impressive succession of Projecting Lips that I have yet encountered is to be found in the Young Men's Christian Association's hall in Halifax (now used for many purposes, and not necessarily confined to those who are young, or male, or of one particular faith in preference to another). It spurns the easy option of a lift. To reach the main hall, in all its balconied splendour, it is necessary for the Young Christian Men, yourself and others to ascend thirty-seven steps from street level. Of this number, no less than twenty-seven have projecting lips, repeated in a second matching staircase, all in solid stone: a formidable challenge to all comers.

But such sterling independence of character is the very hallmark of Halifax, where the grey-stone buildings are carved out of the steep valley-sides, and the double-decker buses sail high in the night sky, well clear of the speaker and his puny struggles in the valley below.

 **is also for OLD BOYS**

Old Boys, by their very nature, have not seen each other for a very long time, and therefore have plenty to talk about. They could easily do without an after-dinner speaker, but they courteously give him a hearing, and invite him to join them for their meal before he speaks.

The convivial meal continues until late, and is followed by further conviviality, succeeded by speeches and less formal reminiscences and anecdotes.

It is therefore not far short of midnight when the speaker rises to his feet. He finds that his audience is now noticeably smaller, as the oldest of the Old Boys have set off on their unsteady way home. This leaves what might be called the Hard Core, and the speaker receives vocal demands to elaborate upon aspects of his subject that would normally go beyond the bounds of what is considered respectable. Eventually, the next day having begun, his somewhat protracted dissertation draws to an end, and the reunion begins to unreunion itself.

On one such occasion I found myself packing-up my equipment in restricted circumstances, as the area around my screen, which I was trying to collapse, was already occupied by Old Boys who had already done so. I had therefore to reach awkwardly across the space between an Old Boy and an upright piano, which I think had been used some hours earlier for the accompaniment of Old Boys' songs, which had not included Jerusalem.

By some misjudgment I lost my feet, and hit my head (which has no natural protection) against the top corner of the piano. It was not a heavy blow – no more than one would normally expect at that hour of an Old Boys' reunion – and, having found my feet again, I continued to grapple with my screen.

Various Old Boys came up to continue chatting with me about this and that, and I made a point of trying to see them all. But then I realized that I was not seeing any of them clearly. I put it down to the heat of the room and the lateness of the hour. With the back of my hand I brushed aside something in my eye, while the next of the Old Boys was wishing me well. He continued his friendly farewell.

We were about to shake hands when I noticed that my right hand was covered in blood. So, I then discovered by the blood-soaked handkerchief test, was my head.

Clearly, the Old Boys were not deterred by the sight of blood. Indeed, they did not allow it in any way to deflect their conversation while, without referring to it, they bade me farewell. I completed my packing with one hand, the other holding my bloodstained handkerchief to staunch the flow.

Only the treasurer and I were left. He approached me with considerable concern. Perhaps, I thought, he was going to offer me a clean handkerchief.

'You don't want a fee' he said, succinctly, '*do you.*' (See FEES).

It was not the time of night for debate. Earlier that evening the Head had invited contributions to the Old School Minibus Fund. I now suggested that my previously agreed fee be paid into this fund by the Old Boys.

With only faintly-discernible chagrin on the part of the conscientious treasurer, my suggestion was accepted, and we went our respective homeward ways.

This display of *sang-froid* in the face of bloodshed had a remarkable echo a year or two later, after I had been speaking to an entirely different audience in a very different place.

The audience – members of a distinguished lecture society – had drifted away, leaving only the chairman and myself to let ourselves out of the building. It was a pitch-black night as we emerged into the unlit car-park. Suddenly, as we were chatting, the silence was rent with screams of distress. They were coming from the far end of the car park.

'*He-e-lp, he-e-lp*' cried a woman's voice, and we rushed towards the source of the disturbance. We found an unfortunate lady member of the audience on her knees, with her face and clothes covered in blood.

'I must have tripped up,' she cried. 'I think I've broken my nose!'

The chairman and I helped her to her feet, and I gave her a clean handkerchief to staunch the flow, while we uttered words of sympathy and consolation. There was no one else to be seen.

Having made sure that she had sufficiently recovered, we helped the victim to her car, which throughout was standing alongside, with the driver's window lowered and the engine ticking over. She got into the passenger seat, and the car was driven off into the night.

It wasn't until later that the thought struck me forcibly: *Who was driving the car?*

He must have been an Old Boy.

☆　　☆　　☆

 **is for PARKING**

I suppose that the difficulties of parking one's car are no greater for the speaker than for any other citizen. They merely seem to be.

For one thing, the ordinary citizen does not normally carry two hundredweight of essentials around in his boot. For another, the ordinary citizen does not have an anxious speaker-finder expecting his arrival ten minutes ago. You therefore park as close as you lawfully can, and sometimes unlawfully.

This is seldom a problem where an evening meeting is involved. The rest of the world has already gone home when you arrive, and your audience, if any, will not be turning up for another half-hour. You can therefore expect to have the pick of parking places, whether in a public car-park, or on a private forecourt, or in the best corner of the nearest cow-pasture.

But daytime meetings, especially those in city-centres, are a very different kettle-of-fish. When you arrive, the rest of the world has already been occupying the only parking spaces all morning.

You may of course try to pose as a deliverer of goods, in an attempt to share the immunity extended to all those goods vehicles which bask with impunity on the double yellow lines outside your destination. But since you have no hope of persuading the authorities that you are unloading casks of beer, you will have to signal by other means your alleged role as a deliverer.

The use of hazard flashers cannot be relied upon: you are merely saying to the traffic warden: 'I know I'm sinning, but only a little.' Unloading is sure to take you more than ten

Leeds University

Forming a strange visual partnership with its neighbouring begrimed Victorian rows of houses, the distinctive white tower of the University's Parkinson Building (1949) soars above all else: even the nearby Town Hall. There are no awkward staircases here for the speaker: he is swept aloft in a choice of lifts, into a clinical, tiered lecture theatre. By contrast, in the background rises the black spire of St George's Church. In its crypt, manned mainly by volunteers, the church has for 60 years been caring for the homeless and the rootless.

minutes, and I have been booked by a warden when my sin – not even an enjoyable one – has been lasting for less than five minutes.

An alternative signal of alleged innocence is to leave your boot lid wide open. This tells the warden that you are a disingenuous fool, and he may extend to you the tolerance sometimes allowed to the well-intentioned nitwit. The problem here is that you may return to find that nothing is left in the boot for you to unload.

Even if your short-term-unloading ploy succeeds, you will still be required to drive elsewhere to park afterwards. In some cities – I have in mind Leeds and Lancaster in particular – the nearest multi-storey car-park can be within a stone's throw, but require a mile's drive around the city's one-way system to get there. By the time you return on foot to your destination, your audience will have forgotten that they were expecting you.

Sometimes therefore you have no alternative but to do the Long Haul. To illustrate what can happen, I must now recount my experience when due to speak to members of the Women's Gas Federation.

Until a couple of years ago, I went through life in ignorance of the existence of this distinguished organization. But I am now happily enlightened. An interesting information leaflet explains that the Federation had its origins in the 1930s, in the form of what were then termed Ladies' Gas Circles. If their progress in those days was circuitous, it no longer is: the Federation's slogan is now WOMEN GOING FORWARD.

It was to be expected that my first invitation to speak to one of the Federation's branches should have come from the dignified and attractive town of Harrogate: Harrogate is the fount of a wealth of organizations, all thirsting for enlightenment, and I suspect liberally lacing it with enjoyment, too.

Indeed, I greatly enjoyed my meeting with the Harrogate Gas Ladies, who were as hospitable and receptive a group as I have

107

known, even though my contribution to their enlightenment included only one picture of a gas lamp. It was no fault of theirs that the hotel in which we convened was desperately short of car-parking space (Harrogate having been built in the days when everyone arrived by train). To my dismay I could find no place to park near the entrance of the hotel, nor anywhere else in the hotel car-park, nor in the surrounding or even more distant streets. I ended up in the multi-storey car park, which was some ten minute's walk away.

This wouldn't have mattered had I merely had to walk back to my venue. But I also had to make my three journeys with my equipment (see **OBSTACLE**), two of them with my sack-barrow.

No longer do many visitors arrive at Harrogate by train. Clearly the inhabitants regarded with suspicion the sight of what they took to be loaded station luggage-wheels being wheeled by a quasi-respectable citizen through the streets of the town, far from the confines of the railway station.

But not so the lady in the hotel, just arrived from the USA. When she saw me as I entered the hotel lobby, she cried triumphantly, 'Oh, porter, when you've gotten rid of those, will you take these three bags of mine to room 302?'

I had to decline, on the grounds that when I had gotten rid of my load, involving two further journeys in the elevator to the fourth floor, I had to deliver a talk to seventy-five waiting Federated Ladies of Gas. It was clear that she did not believe this lame excuse from an uncooperative member of the hotel staff.

☆   ☆   ☆

By contrast, in anticipation of parking difficulties, your hosts may sometimes notify you that they have been able to arrange for a special parking-space to be saved for you. Such was the case when I arrived at a former coaching inn on what used to be called the Great North Road.

The inn happened to be in the centre of a busy and congested city. The excellent city-map with which I had been provided indicated exactly the position of the hotel's car park entrance. To reach it, one had to drive into the very teeth of an adverse one-way street, before turning sharply left into a narrow entrance-way, which disappeared within the hotel building itself.

On reaching this point of no return, I found my way blocked by another car, with no one in it. Taking the risk of leaving mine with its rear projecting into the adverse one-way street, I walked ahead to spy out the land.

In front of the abandoned car was another. And another. And another. Far beyond the line of abandoned cars lay the hotel entrance, within what was clearly the covered former coaching-

109

yard. There was no hope whatever of reaching the entrance with my car to unload it, nor indeed of parking it anywhere at all. Nor could I simply turn round and go away.

I put my problem to the receptionist.

'I'll get the porter,' she said.

'But a porter's no good,' I protested, 'I don't want anybody to *carry* anything. I need to get my car in.'

'The porter will move the cars,' she stated icily.

I hurried out to stand by my own car, only to find two policemen already doing so. They listened to my problem with scepticism, and firmly insisted that I must remove it immediately.

'This one-way street's a double-decker bus lane,' said one.

'They shoot through it like a bat out of hell' said the other.

'They'll take the back off your car like a dose of salts,' added the first.

With these alarming figures of speech ringing in my ears, I was allowed to reverse temporarily on to double yellow lines, with hazard-lights flashing. I could only hope desperately against hope that the porter would quickly achieve his single-handed, superhuman task of pushing the cars ahead of me out of the way.

After twenty agonizing minutes, the porter at last appeared. He summoned my car into the miraculously cleared inner forecourt, from which I was able to unload direct into the reception area.

'How did you manage that?' I asked him.

He held up two bulging handfuls of keys.

'Easy,' he said. 'Everybody has to leave their car keys at reception. I'll have to have yours now, please.'

None of the keys, including mine, were labelled or otherwise identified.

I was reminded of the mixed party-game where everyone tosses their key (or shoe, or whatever) into a heap on the floor, the heap is stirred, and after a general scrabble the owner takes the finder as her partner. Eyeing the foyer, which was crowded with elegant ladies in eloquent conversation, I began to wonder what

Pateley Bridge

To get in and out of Pateley Bridge, you have to swoop down one steep side of lovely Nidderdale, and up the other even steeper side. But you will of course stop at the bottom, because this attractive village is the reason why you came here. Perhaps you have come to speak to the thriving Nidderdale Society, whose 100 and more members meet in the excellent Memorial Hall, near the bottom of the hill. (To be fair to all, they also meet alternately six miles down the Dale, in the Dacre Village Hall).

111

lay in store for me.

But alas, the game had no reward for the owners of the keys, apart from having their cars manoeuvred by the porter into the most inaccessible corners of the courtyard to make way for others. After years of experience, the friendly porter had become an expert matcher of anonymous keys with unknown cars, by the skilful process of trial and error.

There must be easier, and perhaps more exciting, ways of dealing with hotel visitors' parking problems.

☆　　☆　　☆

It's frustrating enough to be unable to park when there is no parking space available. But it's worse to be denied space in the midst of plenty. One dark, wet night I arrived at the approaches to the imposing civic building in which I was to speak. In front of it was an expansive and well-lit car park, the entrance to which was coned-off. It was totally empty. I left my car at its entrance, and walked the 100 yards or so to the entrance-portals of the building. The door attendant was expecting me, but not my car.

'Sorry,' he replied firmly to my request to remove the cones so that I could drive up to unload outside the portals. 'You can't come into this car-park. You'll have to park over there.'

He indicated an adjoining car-park, several hundred yards in another direction. I asked him whether the area in which we were standing was required for other purposes for the few minutes during which I would be unloading.

'No,' he said, indicating cars being driven into the other car-park, 'but just look at all that lot arriving. They're coming here tonight too, you know. If I let *you* bring your car in here, they'll *all* want to be in here.'

I was clearly not to be allowed this privilege. My car and I were instead expelled to the great Equal Society of the distant outer car park, from which I had to push my loaded sack-barrow twice, each time under the satisfied scrutiny of the door attendant. Meanwhile, the expansive car-park in front of the building remained proudly empty throughout the evening. Civic officialdom had triumphed.

In complete and heartening contrast, I prefer to savour the uniquely helpful treatment that I enjoyed in a certain city some 100 miles to the west. I had purposely arrived outside the speaking-place in mid-afternoon, so that I could explore the city on foot for a few hours before speaking in the evening. Though I knew its waterways well, I was unfamiliar with its car-parks, of which I could see none, other than a single half-hour space.

A traffic warden was walking by. I explained my circumstances, and asked her advice as to where to park for some two or three hours.

'Here you are,' she said, pointing to the half-hour space.

'Well, thanks very much,' I replied lamely. 'But I'm afraid that won't be long enough for me.'

'Don't you argue,' she countered sternly, 'you'll be all right. *I'm the boss around here!'*

And so she was, as evidenced by the absence of a parking ticket when I returned to my car two hours later. It was the parking experience of a lifetime.

No, I'm sorry. I'm *not* going to tell you where . . .

Bishop Burton

Bishop Burton has the largest and most attractive village pond in what was, and should soon again be, Yorkshire. It also has one of the country's leading agricultural colleges (hidden behind the trees). Here is an excellent conference hall, well-used by local organisations to raise money for good causes. Close by is the curiously-named Altisidora Inn (seen above) in which the speaker can find refreshment before and/or after such thirst-creating events.

 **is also for POINTER**

We must now become highly technical.

Every now and again when your slides are being projected, you may feel the need to attract the attention of your audience to what you are talking about. It might be the room of the hotel in which you stayed in Ashby-de-la-Zouche, or your neighbour's rottweiler, or the district councillor whose back is turned to the camera.

You can of course walk up to the screen and point with your hand. This is not always easy. You may forget that the screen is on the stage and you are not. Having reached the screen, you may find that what you want to point at is out of reach. On turning back towards the projector you may be dazzled by the brilliance of your own picture, and your audience sees only your silhouette before, unable to see where it is going, it disappears from the screen and on to the floor of the house.

A more sophisticated approach is to use a **pointing-pole.** This can be long, heavy, and useful for emphasis (see REMOTE CONTROL) or it may, as is sometimes used in business seminars, be **telescopic**. This enables the businessman to carry it everywhere in his inside-pocket, so that he can point out anything to anyone at any time. But in either case, because the end of the pointer impacts against the screen, the picture may be punctured.

It is here that the 'hands off' pointer comes into its own. By this device one can project an illuminated shape on to the screen: sometimes an arrow, sometimes a hairpin. It will show up excellently on a blank, darkened screen, but its feeble image tends to disappear from view when a picture appears.

It was therefore a rare privilege to find myself one evening

115

offered the experience of using the secret weapon of the Speaking World: a **laser pointer** (see NECKWEAR).

To operate this device, you hold a small black box in your hand, press a red button, and suddenly a brilliant, searing red dot hits the screen. You can pinpoint with total accuracy the window of your room in Ashby-de-la-Zouche, the ear of the district councillor, and the eyeball of the rottweiler. Or you can aim your laser beam at the EXIT sign, or the flowers on the piano, or twirl it in interesting patterns around the ceiling.

You learn for the first time what it's like to be able to shoot from the hip.

And so to its paramount feature: The instructions warn you *never to point the laser at yourself or the audience.* I believe that this is in case someone falls down dead.

Bearing in mind its various possible uses, I have, at considerable cost, managed to obtain a laser pointer for my personal use (see GIFTED CHILD).

 **is also for PROJECTOR**

Forget for the moment your laser pointer, which arrived first only by a trick of the alphabet.

As a slide-speaker, you will have to make a big decision: are you going to use your hosts' projector, which they are convinced is better than your own? If you do, you must take the risk, as recounted earlier (see BREAKDOWN), that you may be faced with one or two local difficulties.

To reduce the element of risk, I always take my own projector with me as a standby, and I would recommend you to do the same. What kind of projector should you possess?

You must first decide whether you are going to be a Carousel-Man/Woman or a Magazine-Man/Woman.

This has little to do, as you may think, with fairground life or male or female modelling. It has everything to do with how much control you have over your own slides.

As the name implies, a CAROUSEL PROJECTOR'S slides go round and round. You fit them beforehand into the carousel, which looks rather like the underside of a large plastic mushroom, and clamp a cover on top. The carousel, slides and all, is then clamped into the projector. Most carousels then go round horizontally like a roundabout, though some rotate vertically like the Big Wheel.

As in the fairground, whatever goes into the carousel has to go round. Once the roundabout starts, there's no getting off until the ride has finished.

This means that you have to decide beforehand precisely which slides go on to the roundabout. You also have to decide in what position they will travel. Once they start, you cannot

117

control whether they will be right way up, upside down, wrong way round or out of order.

This is why the carousel-projector audience may sometimes experience a fairground-like sensation, when slides appear in unintended and irremedial disorder. The audience must then lie on its side or stand on its head.

It has been known for a lecturer's entire carousel collection to be projected upside down, leaving the exhausted audience in disarray, while the lecturer (a professor, upright) calmly continued his commentary.

For similar reasons, if the speaker has accidentally inserted a carousel of slides on the wrong subject, he must inexorably go through with it. He may do this by proceeding at dizzy speed through all eighty slides (the standard load for a carousel) without bothering to comment, as has been known. Or he may adapt his commentary to the slides, even though it is not what the audience came to see.

I heard recently of a speaker who arrived at the lecture hall with his carousel, only to find that it contained no slides. He had accidentally picked up the wrong carousel. Rather than treat his audience to an extempore dissertation, he decided to go and get his slides, come what may. While the audience waited, he drove forty miles along winding roads in forty minutes flat. I understand that while members of the audience were waiting, the chairman regaled them with his *own* account of what the speaker was intending to say, and the purpose of this heroic drive was largely frustrated.

We must resume our examination of the carousel projector. One advantage is that it often possesses another fairground characteristic: this is technically known as **the Long Throw**. This means simply that it can throw a picture all the way from the back of the hall to the front, whether the picture be right way round, sideways or upside down. By the time it hits the screen it will be much bigger. By and large, therefore, a carousel projector is likely to be preferable for the larger audience of, say, 150 people or more.

But the Long Throw has the disadvantage that the projector is a long way away from the speaker, and well beyond his personal control. Even with an efficient remote control (of which more later), the speaker is still dependent upon someone else to change from one carousel to another, and to step in in case of breakdown, mechanical or human (see BREAKDOWN).

By contrast, the MAGAZINE PROJECTOR often has a modest throw of not more than twenty feet. In circumstances other than luncheon clubs it sits on a stand in the centre aisle, and is usually easily accessible to the speaker. The magazine is in every sense more straightward. As you might expect, it moves straight forwards as the slides go in and out – none of your dizzy fairground antics.

But the most important advantage of the magazine is that you can get at the slides at any time you like. If a slide happens to be upside down you can eject and replace it correctly after no more than four attempts. If by some mischance you have inserted a whole magazine of pictures of the Forth Bridge instead of

119

studies of garden lilies, you can remove the Forth Bridge instantly and switch to your lilies. Moreover, you can edit as you go along, missing out individual and even whole blocks of slides.

The facility to reduce the length of your talk is essential in a number of varying circumstances:

(a) When your hosts have already asked you in advance to do so.
(b) When you are late getting started because of over-running important preceding business (e.g. see OLD BOYS).
(c) When a slide is unsuitable for exhibition to your present audience
(d) When your audience is restive.
(e) When you audience is getting up and going.
(f) When the building is on fire.

It will now be no surprise to you that my own projector is of the magazine type.

If I use a carousel projector, it is because my hosts prefer it and provide it. In these circumstances I try to let them know well in advance that I shall need three carousels into which to transfer my slides beforehand. When confirming my needs in writing I have to check my spelling, and again reach for Collins:

'CAROUSEL: another name for merry-go-round'
'CAROUSAL: a merry drinking party'

On one such occasion I must have mis-spelt my desires. The reply from the secretary confirming the booking ended:
    'PS. We will let you have three carousals when you arrive.'
Somehow we survived this succession of merry drinking parties before I even started to speak, and the carousal-operator managed to carry out his task with gusto.

☆   ☆   ☆

120

 **is for QUEUE**

After having taken so long over my Ps, I will keep the Qs very brief.

I have already accounted for one queuing experience (see KEY), whereby I found myself queuing to hear myself speak.

The other memorable queue in which, as speaker, I took part was after lunch at an event attended by 350 members of the North Yorkshire West Federation of Women's Institutes. I found myself joining the second of two queues. The first queue, entirely of ladies, was for the ladies' conveniences. The second, also entirely of ladies, and just as long, was for the gentlemen's.

For the first time in my life in this field of human endeavour I had to accept *forces majeures* and find an alternative, and I will not say where.

☆   ☆   ☆

GENTLEMEN

 **is for RELIEF**

(The last item should rightfully have come under this heading. But Q was a difficult letter, and I had no alternative, not having enjoyed, so far as I know, the presence among my audiences of Her Majesty the Queen).

It is prudent for the speaker to ensure beforehand that he can stay the course of his own talk. I did hear of one who did not, and nipped out and back without his listeners being aware that he was missing. But that is pushing too far one's confidence in the somnolence of the audience. As they say, better safe than sorry.

That is why, shortly before I was due to speak at an event to raise money for the building fund of a rural Methodist chapel, I asked the organizer where I could find the Gents. She was uncomfortable and apologetic.

'Oh, dear,' she said, 'that's why we need money for the building fund. We haven't got one.'

I asked her where she would suggest I went. By now other ladies had joined in the discussion. One had a brainwave.

'There's Mabel's up the road,' she said. 'She won't mind.'

I asked where Mabel's was, and she led me outside into the dark night.

'There! she said, pointing to a dim light flickering from a cottage in the distance. 'That's Mabel's.'

I weighed up the distance involved – perhaps half a mile for the return journey – along with the time available and my own staying-power. I was about to abandon the whole proposition when I caught sight of the village pub on the other side of the road.

'It's all right,' I said, 'I'll nip in the pub.'

This suggestion caused consternation among my hearers.

Was it because I proposed to enter a place in which the demon alcohol was purveyed? Or because they thought it unfair that I should use its facilities without buying a drink? I never discovered; but whatever the reason, our discussion seemed to be getting us nowhere.

But then one lady had a sudden insight.

'You *can* go into the pub,' she said, 'It'll be quite all right.'

Her friends looked at her in astonishment, obviously fearful that she had deserted the cause. But confidence flooded back as she explained: 'I've just remembered that the pub management has changed hands. The new manager is a Methodist!' So I was allowed to nip into the pub and the manager was happy to allow me the free use of his facilities without insisting that I bought a pint, even though I wouldn't have minded one had time allowed.

There followed one of the many happy evenings that I have enjoyed with Methodist audiences.

I still wonder however what would have happened, had the pub manager not been a Methodist.

Unfortunately, some time later I was to cause similar embarrassment to Methodist hosts, for a related reason. On this occasion it was explained to me that there was both a Ladies' and a Gentlemen's on the premises, but that the Gentlemen's was not fit for a Gentleman like me to use.

I was therefore escorted, by a lady, through the many side-rooms and corridors that characterize urban Victorian Noncon-formist establishments. At last we arrived at the sought-for-door, where I was left to my own devices. On the door was a notice:

LADIES
THIS TOILET IS ONLY FOR THE USE OF
MEMBERS OF THE CHAPEL

Not being a member of the chapel, I was all the more

appreciative of the twofold dispensation that I was about to enjoy. But I had to put myself in the shoes of any lady who, having managed to find her way to this remote outstation, might have to confess to herself that she was not a member of the chapel. Should she retrace her steps and search elsewhere?

If she didn't, then who would know, apart from God?

For that matter, I wondered, would He really mind?

Let us now move to the other end of the spectrum.

I was to speak at the most splendid country seat in which it has ever been my privilege to set foot as a speaker. The private driveway, nearly a mile long, led through expansive woodland and parkland to a gracious Georgian mansion of warm stone, set beside a river winding idyllically through a valley among trees and water-meadows.

This event also was for fund-raising purposes, and I will not say here what for, except that all political parties have to raise funds somehow, and I try to accommodate those who are needy enough and kind enough to invite me to come.

My talk was to be given in the carpeted coach-house, fitted out for an audience of 100. Before we were ushered there from the stately drawing-room and hall, I took the liberty of putting my usual request to our gracious hostess. 'Yes, certainly,' she said, waving nonchalantly upwards, 'you'll find plenty of bathrooms upstairs.' So I made my way up the spacious staircase and into the tastefully decorated splendour of the bedroom wing. Silently, for such was the luxury of the white carpeting, I searched for one of the bathrooms, but could find none.

Every door led into a bedroom, each in immaculate order with deep and comfortable bed and matching furnishings, but none with what I was looking for. I retreated guiltily: who was I to obtrude upon this privacy?

I then became aware that other people were entering bedrooms with much less hesitation than I, while yet more were emerging with expressions verging on the complacent. Perish the thought – was this fund-raising event a cover for something rather less respectable?

Finally I summoned up the courage to ask for guidance from

one of the guests emerging from a bedroom. Without a word, she led me into and through the bedroom, opened a door, and revealed what I had been seeking – or rather, considerably more, as the spacious room's fittings also included bidet, shower and circular bath with taps, gold.

'They're all *en suite,* you know,' she commented with just a hint of wonder at my ignorance. I felt ashamed that I should ever have thought otherwise. Suitably chastened, I returned to my place in the carpeted coach-house.

☆　　☆　　☆

 **is also for REMOTE CONTROL**

In olden days (that is, when I was at boarding school) the Lantern Lecturer for our compulsory Saturday night entertainment would stand beside the screen with a long and heavy pole, pointed at one end and blunt at the other. He (or very occasionally she) would use the pointed end to point at the screen, and the blunt end to thump the stage. When the stage was thumped, whoever was operating the lantern – a hot, heavy, spitting and crackling monster in whose bowels sparked a carbon arc – was expected to remove the old slide and insert the new one, by hand.

This worked tolerably well, unless the speaker was dramatically inclined.

I well remember a gesticulatory and choleric visiting speaker losing his temper in front of the whole school because the slides were repeatedly changed when he was unready. The more choleric the speaker became, the more he thumped, and the more rapidly were the slides changed. As the luckless operator that night, I could not distinguish between a thump for a slide change and a thump for emphasis. I was never again required to do the job of operator.

A slightly more sophisticated means of signalling to the operator was the CLICKER. This consisted of a spring metal tongue attached to the inside of another piece of metal, usually painted to look like a frog or toad, and sometimes found in Christmas crackers. The speaker concealed it in the palm of his hand, to create the illusion that he was an expert finger-flicker. The clicker was less subject to emotional misuse than the pole-thump, but by its very nature it was apt to spring out of the palm of the hand of the speaker and get lost in the darkness.

Though the carbon arc has long disappeared, there are still projectors on the market which can be controlled only from the projector itself. You can operate one if you like, by standing at the projector and changing the slides yourself, and getting in the way of, and with your back to, half your audience. Alternatively, you can have a stick and thump the floor for someone else to do the slide changing when they think you're not intending to be dramatic; or you can get yourself a clicker.

In the course of time, I'd forgotten how to use a clicker until I was issued with one recently, as the signal to the projectionist of an otherwise excellent hand-operated projector. It was neither a frog nor a toad, but a crocodile. For the first ten slides, it clicked. It then went into hibernation, or whatever. I found that a 10p piece, tapped smartly on the table, produced as efficient a result, with less fearsome trappings.

As the answer to the foregoing problems, man invented the REMOTE CONTROL.

In theory at least, this device enables you, at the press of a button, from wherever you are, smoothly and silently, without getting in anyone's way, to change the slide at the moment of your own choosing.

There are two main types of remote control. The first is on one end of a length of wire, the other end of which plugs into the projector. Taken straight from one to the other, this lead will act as an effective trip-wire for your arriving audience. You therefore run it behind central heating pipes, round the back of pictures, over the tops of doorways and under rows of chairs. It needs to be very long indeed.

Sometimes even a long lead can be embarrassingly short, as I discovered at a meeting of the Bessacarr Ladies' Luncheon Club (which happens to meet in a well-appointed hotel close to a well-known racecourse, though that has nothing to do with it).

It was another of those occasions on which I had set everything up, only to have to take it down again because of violations of the Health and Safety at Work Act. Once again I had to put into action my contingency plan, that is, of doing everything all over again after the serving of coffee. Eventually all was in place except my remote control lead, which I planned to drape around the walls before taking it between the tables to the projector.

But the room was of unique and challenging configuration.

Despite its length, my remote control cable was six feet too short for the discreet route that I had planned. The only way was the direct one, along the floor beneath the first four successive rows of luncheon ladies and their eighty legs.

In some desperation now, but ready to do anything in the name of duty, I took off my jacket, rolled up my sleeves, dismissed my inhibitions and prepared to crawl under the tables towards the projector, remote control wire in hand.

It was at this moment that the nearest lady, clearly having read my intentions, surprisingly took charge.

'Give it to me!' she said.

I protested that this was not her job, but she insisted. I waited for her to get down on her hands and knees. Instead she took the end of the wire, and reached under the table. The lady opposite her, deep in conversation, suddenly straightened up, startled.

'Take it and pass it on!' instructed the first lady, reaching further under the table . . .

The process was repeated, with the ladies of Bessacarr passing the unseen remote control wire from hand to hand and knee to knee. The under-table movement progressed steadily toward the projector, like the wavelet of a water-vole. Finally, like a footballer acclaiming his goal, the lady nearest to the projector held the end of the wire triumphantly aloft. Never has any remote control been worked through so many hands and around so many legs, and never have my slides changed with such sweet smoothness as they did that day.

In view of my Bessacarr experience, and not wishing to push my luck, I decided to change my projector to one with the second type of remote control.

This requires *no wire at all*. In your hand is a ray-gun (not to be confused with the laser pointer), which directs an invisible infra-red ray at the projector. At the press of a button, you can send invisible instructions via its pop-up periscope. You can bring on the next slide, or go back to the last, or make the picture go totally out of focus in either direction. (Unless, that is, the head of that tall chap sitting between you and the projector is in the way. The beam, I have discovered, will not normally pass through the human brain).

By a strange coincidence, I was again at a luncheon club

meeting associated with a racecourse. This time it was nearer home, with the ladies of the York Tuesday Luncheon Club, and I had my new infra-red device. Gone, I thought, were my control problems. My equipment was all shipshape and in place, amid the ample space of the gracious and airy banqueting hall of the Gimcrack Rooms – no need here to infringe the Health and Safety at Work Act. I was able to relax over my lunch in excellent company.

I was looking forward to using my new, invisible infra-red ray.

I should explain here that apart from operating the projector from the front of the audience by remote control, I have to operate a tape recorder from the same point. This in turn produces occasional sounds and music through a pair of speakers in either corner of the room. It gives the audience a periodic rest from my voice, and affords me an opportunity to take a swig at whatever thirst-quenching liquid has been provided (see DRINK).

All of this vital equipment – tape-recorder, torch, laser pointer, infra-red ray and drink – is assembled on a table to the side of the screen, far enough forward for me to be able to see what I should be talking about.

The layout of the banqueting hall required that the projector, ready to receive its infra-red commands, was positioned amid many rows of dining tables and guests. I said my few words of introduction, the lights went down perfectly on cue, the sounds began, and I activated the infra-red command for the first slide.

Nothing happened.

I repeated the commands again and again, and still nothing happened. Meanwhile the music and sounds were stepping merrily on their way, and the proceedings degenerated into confusion before they had even begun.

In retrospect, I realize that I should have called for a volunteer from the audience to act as manual operator at the projector itself, using the 10p piece technique as a command system. I'm sure that a very able lady would have been forthcoming. But unwisely, I decided to man the manual control myself. To do this I had to leave my control-table and take up station beside the projector, in the midst of the forward ranks of my audience. I couldn't stand, for I'd have been blocking the view of the audience beyond. I couldn't sit, as there was nothing to sit on.

So I had to kneel to speak, facing the audience, with head just above table-level.

This would have worked had I been able to remain in that position. But the sound-control was still out in front, and needed to be dealt with at critical moments. It was necessary therefore to keep rising from my knees and sprinting round to the front – a considerable distance in that spacious room – to start the sound; then back to the projector to keep the pictures going; then back to the front to stop the sound; and so *ad infinitum.*

The audience was remarkably tolerant of these distractions, and proceedings eventually reached their breathless end.

As for the invisible infra-red ray, which had been so invisible that even the projector couldn't spot it, I later returned it with suitable protest to the manufacturers. They apologetically replaced it, and it has shone, invisibly, ever since.

But now I know the real meaning of the expression *On Your Knees,* and I keep my 10p at the ready.

Church House, Ilkley

It is perhaps ironic that Ilkley, or rather its Moor, should provide the setting for Yorkshire's only recognisable, and cannibalistic, folk-song, versions of which are still rendered by supporters of Leeds United. For Ilkley is the epitome of respectability, and nowhere more so than in Church House, in the far corner of this quiet little cobbled courtyard, well hidden from the main road from West Yorkshire to the Lake District. Here meets the only Professional and Business _Ladies_' Club that I have yet had the pleasure of encountering (but their menfolk came, too).

 **is for SCREEN**

If your talk is accompanied by slides (or vice versa), members of your audience have a right and expectation to be able to see what it is that you are talking about, without physically contorting themselves (see **PROJECTOR**). The size and shape of the screen are therefore critical. Let us deal first with shape.

Virtually all slides are oblong. Of these, some are across and others straight up ('landscape' and 'portrait' respectively, to use the trade's jargon). If therefore you are to project your slides as God intended – that is, with the horizon from side to side and waterfalls from top to bottom – your screen needs to be as high as it is wide, in other words square. Unfortunately this means that whenever a slide is projected on the screen, one-third of the screen is unavoidably wasted.

A rectangular screen wastes still more. By a process of arithmetic, with which I will not weary you, you will lose three-fifths of the screen area. Beware, therefore, of your hosts' assurance that they have a 'six-foot-wide screen'. Unless it is equally high, your audience will see a picture the size, apparently, of a postage-stamp. It is therefore a good idea to make sure that your hosts' screen is square, or very large, or both. Otherwise you will have to bring one with you.

The largest 'portable' screen that I have ever encountered was hired for a charity event at which I was to speak, involving a large audience in a large and historic civic building. As the word 'portable' was used in its trade description, I had offered to collect, transport and assemble the screen myself.

For a start, its combined components weighed something like a quarter of a ton, in containers of various sizes. These components comprised a complex network of supposedly interlocking steel frames and braces, which were intended to rise progressively from the floor as they were assembled. The complete frame was about five yards high and five yards wide. To this gigantic structure had to be attached the screen material, held in place by several dozen draw-cords.

Single-handed, I struggled to assemble the flailing pieces of metalwork and flapping sheets. After an hour, I discovered one of its subtle secrets. The framework had to be constructed, not as I had supposed from the bottom upwards, but from the top downwards. The top therefore ended beyond human reach, hoisted ever higher as the bottom progressed.

In short, I could have done with a helping hand.

It was not that I was alone. During my long struggle in this historic setting, I became aware that other people were gathering. They were walking purposefully through the hall carrying folders and briefcases, obviously on a mission of importance. Were they members of the committee organizing this charity event? As they passed by, they greeted my desperate efforts with a friendly smile, and some even wished me good evening.

But helping hand came there none.

I have no doubt that had I actually asked for a hand, it would have been gladly given. But I later discovered that I would have been diverting key resources. For these members of the citizenry were on their way to a different, and much more important, form of public enlightenment: their meeting of the City Council, no less.

The largest easily-portable screen is six feet square. It can be rolled up, unrolled and assembled without calling upon the assistance of city councillors, and stands on its own three feet. It is sufficient for an audience of up to about 150 people.

You will quickly discover however that it must also be adjustable for height, both top and bottom.

If you have to set it up on a stage, which will be frequently, you will have to be able to counteract the additional height of the stage. Otherwise your pictures will be too low. You will then have to tilt the projector upwards, beyond its adjustable limits, requiring piles of coins, blocks of wood or *Hymns Ancient and Modern*.

But tilting the projector can have dire consequences. The magazine, fully loaded with slides, may itself slide backwards and discharge its contents on to the floor. It is then useful to have a senior member of the audience come up and tell his life story, while you sort out any slides that are not cracked, put them in order and try again.

This has happened to me in the past; and I have heard that it has happened to others. One lecture society's favourite horror-story concerned a lecturer of that superior breed which uses not one projector, but two. This means that one picture can be faded into another, so that the audience is unconscious that any change has taken place. The slides are loaded and projected strictly alternately from the two projectors, which sit on top of each other on a common base.

On this occasion the lecturer had to tilt the common base, and the entire contents of both projectors were commonly tipped all over the floor, and not in alternate order. An hour later, the show resumed.

Occasionally you will encounter exceptional screens: the vast theatre screen that descends from above; the screen with myriads of tiny holes to improve reflectability; or – the ultimate – the screen with the great concave curve, to ensure wall-to-wall definition. But these are all large installations, and I doubt if you would get one into your car.

Which leads me now to the workaday matter of transporting the screen, and how, by roundabout circumstances, it nearly led to a rift with my wife.

To transport a six-foot portable screen, one needs at least a hatchback vehicle. I load my screen through the back door of my hatchback along the passenger side, with one end resting on the left-hand end of the dashboard and the other on the back of the rear seat.

In my previous car, it was also necessary to fully recline the front passenger seat to prevent the screen from seesawing on it.

One evening, I had returned home from, shall we say, Cleckheaton, and hurriedly unloaded the car before setting out again for a meeting in our village. The meeting was to be addressed not by me but by a visiting lady speaker. As she did not drive, another member of the audience had brought her. I had offered to drive her home afterwards.

I found it a great pleasure to relax as a member of the audience, able to listen to another speaker, speaking compellingly on a subject totally different from my own.

After the meeting the speaker and I emerged into a wet night and total darkness, our village being free of street lighting. We found our way to the car, and set off. As we drove the fifteen miles to our speaker's home, she continued to speak compellingly, to my privileged ear alone. There were times when I thought that she sounded slightly distant, but otherwise I had no difficulty in hearing her.

We exchanged polite thanks, bade each other goodnight, and I drove home.

My car was unused the following day, but my wife and I had to go out that evening. She got into the car beside me, leaned back, and totally disappeared from view.

My wife still does not believe that I had reclined the passenger seat to accommodate my folding screen at Cleckheaton; that I forgot to straighten it before the subsequent meeting in the village; that the lady lecturer was fully reclined all the way home while speaking to me compellingly; and that I never noticed her posture, nor attempted to do anything about it.

But I have since changed my car, and it is no longer necessary to recline the passenger seat to accommodate my screen. Dammit.

☆　　☆　　☆

 **is also for SEX**

May I make it clear (as I think I have to my wife) that there is no relationship whatsoever between the last topic and this, other than their first letter. Indeed, this subject rears its head now only because of another statistical analysis that I carried out after my study of ENJOYMENT AND OTHERWISE.

I must get to the point before my explanation becomes any more convoluted.

In this analysis, purely for interest, I took out statistics of the sex distribution of my audiences. Here they are:

Mixed-sex audiences: 68%
Audiences of women only: 29%
Audiences of men only: 3%

These markedly unbalanced figures can be interpreted in whatever way you like. Here are some suggested conclusions:

1. My subject is of healthy interest to both sexes
2. It is not of healthy interest to men
3. Women know what is good for them
4. Men do not
5. Men have better things to do with their time
6. Men cannot afford what is good for them.

Before too many conclusions are drawn, however, I must qualify the apparent disinterest of men's organizations in what is good for them. The above figures refer strictly to the composition of the audience, as distinct from the organizers. In practice, many of the mixed-sex events have been organized by men's bodies, or should I say organizations.

I have in mind particularly Rotarians (see ILLUMINATION), to whom I may so far in this dissertation have done less than justice.

Most Rotary clubs, because they meet at lunch-time in between their demanding business and professional affairs, are unable to give the speaker much more than twenty minutes' batting-time. This would mean that, to accommodate me, they would have to re-cast my show as an eight-week soap opera.

Understandably therefore they prefer to get me over-and-done-with at one throw and not for lunch, thankyou. Instead they sometimes organize a members-and-their-ladies social event, or an all-in fund-raising affair. Whichever it may be, the organization, hospitality and bonhomie are always excellent.

Rotarians are also uncommonly perceptive: you can't pull the wool over their finely-tuned rotating antennae. Thus it was no surprise when one Rotary president, in his closing vote of thanks, referred to the speaker as an Extrovert Exhibitionist. At that time of night, and as a sometime Rotarian, I found it an honour to be given due recognition.

The sex distribution figures conceal a further injustice. I have shamelessly categorized all WI and YCW meetings as 'women only', even though husbands have generously been invited to some of these meetings. I apologize to those husbands who have had the goodness to come along: their rarity has made them conspicuous by their presence, which has been all the more appreciated by the speaker. Husbands who attend usually do useful things (see ILLUMINATION and DRINK).

By contrast, the 'men only' meetings are precisely that. You will never see a woman at a statutory men's meeting, because women are never invited (other than to do the washing up, and then only behind the scenes). Perhaps I should insist on equal representation, but somehow I doubt if that would be popular, whether among those who come or those who prefer to stay away.

Finally an afterthought before we leave this subject.

I referred earlier (see ENJOYMENT AND OTHERWISE) to the hard work and dedication of countless groups in voluntary fund-raising activities, which form a significant strand in the nation's social fabric.

My observations suggest that, whilst men often make important contributions – both individually and collectively – in the planning and execution of fund-raising projects, the sustained day-to-day effort is carried out mostly by women, either in their own capacity or as their husbands' wives, or both. This is not a criticism of my own sex. It is a natural consequence of the fact that we are out at work all day until we retire or die, and even then some of us spend our time speaking rather than doing good.

I found myself pondering this point on my way home from talking at an excellently organized and successful charitable fund-raising evening. It had been arranged entirely by members of Tangent (the organization for the wives of husbands who, like myself, have become too old at forty to remain in Round Table, and have therefore gone to seed).

Social and legislative pressures all point to the likelihood that increasing numbers of women of all ages and social groups will be continuing in, or resuming, full-time work. They will therefore have less time for daytime or evening fund-raising and social activities.

Conversely, more of their menfolk – whether voluntarily or displaced by Equal Women – are likely to be around, either at home or on the golf-course, during the day.

Will sufficient men be dedicating themselves to voluntary fund-raising activities to compensate for the loss of women? Or will we menfolk have other things to do with our time?

And if the latter is to be the case, what will be the future of voluntary fund-raising as we know it?

Scarborough Castle

Of all the seaside resorts, Scarborough must offer the greatest variety of interest, including its magnificent castle, two bays, the splendid hinterland of the North York Moors, plus Alan Ayckbourn. For speakers who are thankful not to be entirely surrounded by their audience, Scarborough offers also the excellent YMCA theatre, which has a <u>wrap-around screen</u>. What less could we expect from the characteristically efficient fund-raising activities of the local Rotary?

East Keswick

On our boyhood expeditions from Headingley, pushing our bikes up this steeply-rising main street, the village shop in East Keswick was a vital port-of-call for buying Tizer and sherbert fountains. Then onwards, whizzing down the lanes into Wharfedale. This Keswick is some 80 miles east of its Lakeland namesake. Though now mainly a dormitory village, it retains its character; and its countryside is unspoilt. In its spacious village hall, to the right, meets the local branch of the sturdily independent Yorkshire Countrywomen's Association. They drink tea, not Tizer.

142

 **is for TOFFEE**

I must apologize to all WI members if it appears that I cannot, or will not, leave them alone. Nor can I leave unmentioned Yorkshire's home-rule alternative, the Yorkshire Country-women's Association, at whose meetings the unversed speaker would detect few differences from the WI in the heart, mind and purpose of its members. Indeed, some ladies are happy to be members of both.

If I think of these organizations frequently, it is because they are an essential strand in the rich fabric of our country life, and have a commensurate impact on the life of the speaker. Most branches are too small by themselves to muster my requested minimum audience of sixty; but they usually succeed with flying colours by opening their meetings to members from other branches and to other friends, including sometimes even their husbands (see SEX).

They frequently hold competitions for their members. The theme is usually a simple one, such as a Thriller in Fifty Words, a Photograph of My Neighbour, or a Memory of Manchester. The speaker may be asked to be the judge of the entries, and to rank them in order of first, second, third, and as many more placings as may be required.

The speaker is not required to have any knowledge of the subject on which he is passing judgment. Often, therefore, it is difficult for him to distinguish between the degree of excellence of one entry compared with another. The bold speaker may attempt publicly to justify his judgments, though this will not spare him the unspoken dismay of the disappointed entrants.

Let me take you now to within a stone's throw of the River

143

Nidd, and the village of Killinghall. It has one of the best-appointed and most outstandingly lit village halls that I have come across. It was here that the Killinghall Women's Institute was meeting with its friends.

The date was the last Friday in October: the last meeting before November 5th. I had been warned that there was to be a competition on a theme linked with Guy Fawkes. I expected it to be, say, a Catherine-Wheel Cake, or a Skyrocket of Flowers. But it was neither. The subject was:

BONFIRE TOFFEE

Because this was a Group Meeting of the WI, there were many entries: no less than ten of them, variously arranged and presented, and all in different shapes, sizes and shades of toffee.

This is easy, I thought: Judge them on quality of presentation. I began to scrutinize them under the brilliant illumination, and was getting on quite well when the chairman drew me into a slightly less well-lit area and whispered tactfully:

'I think you'll need to taste it, too.'

It was back to the drawing-board – or rather, the tooth-drawing board. I had to stick my teeth into, then chew, then unstick my teeth, then dispose of, then form a judgment on, one platterful, cartonful and bagful after another of bonfire toffee, bonfire toffee and more bonfire toffee. As I did so I was watched

closely by each of the entrants, to ensure that her entry had a thorough tasting. The results had to be written down on a piece of paper, as I was unable to speak.

Now, at last, I know what good Yorkshiremen really mean when I hear them comment:

'Ee can't talk for bloody toffee.'

Since then, I've avoided any booking in the week before the fifth of November.

 **is for UNFED**

Most ladies' refreshment clubs are luncheon clubs. As we have seen, they ensure that they have their refreshment before the speaker begins to speak.

But some are tea clubs, and it is here that the formula can vary. The speaker may be asked to speak before, after, or even during, tea, according to local custom.

The most interesting tea club timetable, I discovered, was closer to the River Tyne than the River Nidd. As soon as I arrived, not long after lunch, I was asked what I would like for my tea: a hot pie or a cold pie. This question was put to each of the members of the club as they arrived, and the answer carefully recorded.

I busied myself as usual with the equipment with which you are now familiar, and it was some time before I realized that the members were sitting down to tables already set for tea. Furthermore, pies were already being set down on plates in front of them.

On the assumption therefore that my talk would come after tea, I stepped outside for a breath of fresh, Tyneside air. But a little Tyneside air had to go a long way. I was quickly recalled, and informed that I must be ready to start in five minutes' time. Obviously, I decided, this must be a tea club which ate its tea while the speaker spoke: the *Thé Dansant* of the speaking world. So I began to speak.

After a while I became aware, in the reflected light of my slides, that the audience's pies were still there in front of them, untouched. They must be fascinated with my slides, I thought, but they'll soon be tucking in.

But no: still the pies remained untouched and unmoved through slide-change after slide-change, and magazine after magazine. Suddenly I realized the hard truth: *They must all be asleep.*

I decided to take an initiative.

'Don't wait for me – have your tea,' I said loudly, and instantly the audience stiffened.

It is fair to say that they had not awakened from slumber. Instead they were reacting against an assault on their time-honoured tradition, which was explained to me later:

Those who ordered cold pies, got cold pies. They got them before the speaker started. But they were not to touch them until those who had ordered hot pies got theirs, which was after the speaker had finished. This, I learned, made sure that everybody got what they wanted. It stopped people changing their mind, and made sure they didn't forget what they'd ordered.

I realized that I'd forgotten whether I'd ordered hot or cold. But later, on my plate beside the chairman, I found the answer: cold. And very tasty my cold pie was, despite its lonely sojourn while I had been speaking.

☆　　☆　　☆

Some time later, I had a contrasting experience with a certain other club, of whose eating habits I was unsure.

My talk was due to start at 3pm, preceded as I understood it by business at 2.15. Not wishing to interfere with the business, I timed my arrival to set up shop well in advance, after partaking of excellent fare in one of the town's hostelries.

On arrival at 1.30pm, I found to my surprise that tables covered with white tablecloths had been set up throughout the hall. The members were industriously setting them with plates of sandwiches, rolls, salads, cakes, buns, trifles and other substantial goodies, all carefully presented in shrink-wrap.

As this town was also nearer to the Tyne than the Nidd, I decided that this must be a further instance of deferred pleasure, characteristic of the Northern areas of our land. The members were obviously going to have their tea after they had finished with their business and me. I prepared again to compete with the members' anticipation of a good tea while I spoke.

But events were to take a very different turn. At 2.15 prompt, the members took their places at the tables, the chairman's mallet descended, the opening song was sung, and business commenced.

After perhaps five minutes, business ended. Afternoon tea followed at 2.20pm. Replete, I followed at 3pm.

To keep awake, I suspect that my need for the recorded pealing of York Minster Bells was even greater than that of my audience.

☆　　☆　　☆

In conclusion under this heading, I must recount an occasion when, by contrast, the speaker almost went unfed.

The only town in which I've ever had to abandon my car in order to find my speaking-place was Maidstone, Kent. In the dark, its one-way system had totally defeated me by repeatedly despatching me to the outer suburbs whenever I was coming close to my destination. Finally I had to park in the High Street, lights flashing, while I investigated on foot the narrow lane that formed the only lawful approach to where I was expected.

When therefore I eventually arrived with my car, I was far behind schedule. The audience was already beginning to assemble. For reasons that I can explain, but will not here, it consisted mostly of members of the St John Ambulance Brigade. I cannot however explain why it also included a party of Japanese who had landed on these shores two days earlier, for the purpose of improving their English, and I doubt if they benefited much that evening.

But to return to our subject. I was unfed. After unloading and setting up, I hurried off to a nearby Pizza Hut. I asked the waitress whether I could be served quickly, as I had only twenty

minutes before my starting-time of 7.45pm.

'It'll only take a minute,' she said.

At 7.43pm I was served.

I hadn't realized that the waitress had been referring to how long she was giving me to *eat* my pizza. I gulped down one quarter of this large and tasty dish, and offered the substantial remainder to a pale young man with an earring and his girlfriend, who had just finished their meal at the next table.

The young man gratefully accepted the whole of my offering, and immediately set about eating it, despite his girlfriend's vociferous objections. As I rushed out, it looked as though she was preparing to leave him for good.

The rest of the evening, only one minute behind schedule, proceeded without emergency for the St John Ambulance Brigade, and without demur from the Japanese.

But I was saddened that back at the Pizza Hut, for all I knew, I had caused the end of a beautiful friendship in the Garden of England.

The Shire Hall, Howden

You may not have heard of Howdenshire; but the members of the Howden and District Women's Luncheon Club will countenance nothing less: certainly not "Humberside", which they scrupulously omit from their address. To emphasise their independence, they meet in the distinctive Howden Shire Hall. On the opposite side of the attractive Square is Howden Minster, whose splendid square tower dominates the surrounding agricultural landscape and the nearby estuary of the River Ouse.

 **is for VANITY**

We are nearly at the end of our tour of duty, and we must take the opportunity of sounding our trumpet.

After an evening with the Northern Region of the National Association of Flower Arranging Societies (did you know that the Association has 300,000 members throughout the country?) a lady came up to me and kindly and modestly presented me with a sheet of paper.

She had, she explained, heard me speaking at her luncheon club the previous year, and had penned a few lines that I might like to read.

It was not until I got home later that night that I had the chance to take the piece of paper out of my pocket and read it.

On it were twenty-six neatly typed lines of verse, not all of which I shall be vain enough to repeat to you, except to say that I was filled with reassurance. Someone in one of my audiences had been listening to me. Not only that, but she had gone to the trouble of collating the evidence in verse, and with great literary facility, extended even to the courtesy of formal address.

I feel sure that she will not mind if I share with you the following extract:

> *'The resonant voice, poetic words,*
> *the music so in keeping,*
> *The afternoon went swiftly by,*
> *and not a soul was sleeping.*
> *For opening our eyes to see*
> *our city's jewels rare,*
> *We thank you M. W. Jones Esq.*
> *and for your artistic flair.'*

The generosity of this compliment, combined with the need to reveal the truth, encourages me to attempt to reply in suitably chivalrous terms:

ODE TO A LADYE WITH A WELL-KEP'T SECRET

Fair Rhymestress of the Ladyes' Lunching Clubbe!
Who comyth monthly for this joyous Meal
To mete with Friends, and to enjoy the Grubbe
(Much less, to have to hearken to my Spiel):

How can it be that when the Lunching's done
And darkness falls within the Velvet Deepe,
And all fall silent, leaving only One
To Spoute forever: Why cans't thou not Sleepe?

Is't p'raps the Spelle
Of Wond'rous Tayles he Telles?
Not on thy Nellye:
'Tis his Decybelles.

Bulmer Village Hall

The Village Hall, Bulmer

Our well-used village hall shares its history with countless other village halls elsewhere in the land. Over 150 years old, and a Grade II listed building, it was for generations the village school until the population of the village (now 160) became too small to support it. A substantially-constructed building in the Cotswold-type stone found here in the Howardian Hills, it nevertheless needs constant expenditure on maintenance and improvements. The speaker long ago exhausted his captive home-ground audience within, in the name of raising funds for this cause (on whose headed paper this note is penned).

 **is for WIFE**

A wife has certain commitments. They include organizing the local Meals on Wheels; fund-raising in aid of the village hall; forming half of the minority of two ladies on the committee of our local horticultural society; and exercising her energy and skills in the garden whenever the speaker is not engaged in his sole gardening task with the motor-mower.

The speaker's needs are therefore, quite properly, subservient to the above. He does however specify one or two modest requirements, as summarized in the following document that he has prepared for her:

1. TO ENSURE that he remembers his engagements; and to ensure that he forgets nothing else that requires remembering.
2. TO FEED him at whatever hour he requires in order to reach his speaking engagements in time and in the requisite condition.
3. TO PROVIDE him with a freshly laundered and ironed shirt of appropriate specification for each engagement.
4. TO ACCOMMODATE all his equipment in the house when he does not need it, and at all times to help him load it when he does need it, and to unload it when, again, he does not.
5. TO GIVE AND TAKE whatever messages may require attention during his absence, to humour those who require it, and to keep cheerfully at bay those who do not.
6. TO ACCEPT with gratitude his absences, and with toleration his failure to do that which he ought to be doing about the house.

154

7. TO CALM him as necessary, especially when the local evening newspaper falsely bears the following day's date leading him to believe that he has missed that night's engagement.
8. TO WELCOME him home, whatever the hour, with sympathy and sustenance; TO REFRAIN from wearying him with reports of what has been happening in his absence; and TO PAY undivided attention to his account of which letter he has just encountered in the alphabet.

... Which reminds me. I rather think that my wife has forgotten to remind me that she hasn't yet accepted and signed her job description.

☆   ☆   ☆

 **is for CHRISTMAS IS COMING**

When audiences grow weary of listening to speakers, then they can console themselves that Christmas is Coming. For Christmas is the great period of Truce, when audiences all go home, and speakers have no one left to speak to.

The speaker can also go home, to enjoy not being listened to by his family.

☆   ☆   ☆

 **is for YOU**

This catalogue has been written mainly in the first person, solely because it's one person's experience.

Now, it's up to you.

Your catalogue will be very different from mine. But it will be just as varied, and just as unbelievable. You, like me, will have entered a world of surprise, peopled by diverse groups, with a vast range of interests, experience and enthusiasms.

The people one meets enjoy not only each other's company, but also the widening of their horizons. Some are happy, and rightly so, to savour the social pleasures of their group or organization. Others gain their main satisfaction from working hard, usually in their spare time, in support of a wide variety of good causes.

Let us not forget, either, the Reluctant Heroes. They come, not because they really wish to, but through an inborn sense of obligation, or because someone else is twisting their arm. We award them now their Medal of Endurance, before moving on.

Looking in the eye all those members of your potential collective audience, and recognizing their expectations, let us assume that you have been persuaded (entirely of course against your intentions) to enter the speaking world.

How can you minimize misadventure?

My advice would be: don't even try. In the first place, by its nature, you cannot know where or when misadventure will strike next. More important, you would miss all the enjoyment

156

of it, whether at the time or in retrospect.

There are plenty of books on how to be a speaker, and far be it from me to compete with them. You will have learned from my catalogue some of the potential pitfalls.

But here are a few summarized thoughts:

1. Try to chat with at least a few members of your audience beforehand. Then you'll later be able to talk to them as real people, not as any old audience.
   (Be careful, however, not to carry such socializing too far. Once, awaiting the start of a society's preliminary business meeting, I sat on the back row, and fell into interesting conversation with a lady who happened to be unaccompanied. The chairman, admirably socially circulating, arrived at my side. 'Ah!' she said, 'How nice to see you've brought your Good Lady Wife!'

   Fortunately the Good Lady knew how to deal with cases of mistaken identity. A long-standing member of the society, she was a recently retired police officer).

2. Where was I? Ah, yes: Stick to your point.

3. Whatever the difficulties, make yourself heard. If you can't, you and your audience might just as well not be there.

4. Know what you intend to say. If you don't, no one else will.

5. Make sure that, unlike mine, your equipment always works unfailingly; that your slides arc in thc right order, right way round; and that they are in the projector, not all over the floor, and not engulfed in coffee.

6. Always be prepared for the worst.

Let us now look at the demand for speakers, by taking what is grandly known by businessmen as a Global View of the Market. (We exclude, of course, the Pros: the academics, the teachers, the trainers, the politicians and those whose job it is to speak to us on the Sabbath.)

For reasons best known to them, some 250 groups and organizations have kindly included me on their programmes of events. Of these, some 180 meet at least monthly. For me, each occasion has been enjoyably unique. But for the group concerned, I have been just one of an unending succession of speakers, already booked long before I came and went, forgotten, on my way.

From this sample, we work out some interesting arithmetic:

- To fill their programmes, in one year *these organizations alone will have required at least 2,000 talks.*

- But these groups to which I personally have spoken represent only a small proportion of the total of regularly-meeting groups of all sorts in this part of the world. Let us assume that I have encountered one such group in five. In my main catchment area of this North of England sector alone, *we arrive at an annual requirement of 10,000 talks.*

- Projected over the population of the United Kingdom as a whole, *the nation's requirement reaches the formidable total of 100,000 talks per year.*

- This in turn requires *tens of thousands of speakers* to be holding forth at regular intervals throughout the year, on all subjects under the sun.

In a manner of speaking, they and their audiences are all busily developing their own additions to this catalogue of misadventure.

That is why: YOUR COUNTRY NEEDS YOU.

 **is for ZIZZ**

This is what you are now fully entitled to do, unless indeed you're already doing it. You've sat through this talk of mine, the room is warm, your chair is comfortable.

And thank goodness that chap's finished talking his head off.

THE END